A JOURNEY INTO LIGHT

MARIE-ELIZABETH TAYLOR

Copyright © 2013 Marie-Elizabeth Taylor
All rights reserved. No part of this publication may be reproduced, stored in a retrieval system or transmitted, in any form or by any means, without the prior written permission of the author, nor be otherwise circulated in any form of binding or cover other than that in which it is published and without a similar condition being imposed on the purchaser.
ISBN-10: 1483920089
ISBN-13: 978-1483920085

Martin Spencer Israel
1927 - 2007

'The hills and valleys of Heaven will be to those you now experience not as a copy is to an original, nor as a substitute to the genuine article, but as the flower to the root, or the diamond to the coal.'

C. S. Lewis
'Prayer: Letters to Malcolm'

CONTENTS

Acknowledgements

Foreword by Revd Keith Denerley M.A.

Martin Israel: A Short Biography

1.	Passing	17
2.	Coming Home	24
3.	The Group Soul	30
4.	My Own Road to Calvary	49
5.	The Nature of Forgiveness	56
6.	The Deepest Healing	66
7.	Further In	74
8.	The Miracle of the Atonement	83
9.	The Eternal Legacy	89
10.	The Hidden Treasure	94
11.	True Prayer (1)	100
12.	True Prayer (2)	107
13.	The Spirit Filled Life	117
14.	Psychic Sensitivity (1)	125

15.	Psychic Sensitivity (2)	136
16.	Lighting the Path	147
17.	The Conception of Life	165
18.	The Eons of Healing	174
	Notes	187
	Bibliography	191

ACKNOWLEDGEMENTS

Frontispiece photograph of Martin Israel is printed by permission of the Church Times.

Extracts from the works of C. S. Lewis are reproduced by permission of The C. S. Lewis Company Ltd.

The Biblical quotations are all taken from the Revised English Bible unless other sources are mentioned. © Oxford University Press, 1992.

FOREWORD

by the Revd Keith Denerley M.A.

'Guidance from intermediate entities is never to be relied on ... because even a well-intentioned entity is by no means infallible.' (Martin Israel, Smouldering Fire. p89).

When Bess told me that she was in telepathic communication with the President Emeritus of the Churches' Fellowship for Psychical and Spiritual Studies, and that he was (through her) writing a book, my first thought was: 'So they can't keep him quiet!' For on earth Martin had an almost pathological compulsion to write volume after volume. That the apparently dead can communicate from time to time shouldn't surprise those who take Jesus' words in John 11.26 seriously: 'Whoever lives and believes in me shall never die.' Thus St Teresa of Avila continued to receive good advice from St John of the Cross for years after John's passing; and I well remember Bishop Cuthbert Bardsley (who consecrated the new Coventry Cathedral) telling me of a mission service he was taking in Northern Ireland. As he made his way to the pulpit with an address in mind, he distinctly heard the voice of Dorothy Kerin[1] saying: 'Cuthbert, you can't preach that sermon here!' So he didn't. Dorothy had passed from this life several years before.

Now it's always difficult, when considering messages purporting to come from the other side, to know how much is from the originator, and how much from the subconscious of the recipient. I was discussing 'A Testimony of Light' with the Revd. Dr Kenneth Cuming (sometime Chairman of the CFPSS) on one occasion, and he remarked that it was hard to tell how much was genuine Frances Banks, and how much Helen Greaves (see note 1 chapter 3). Suffice to say, perhaps for myself, that having sat at Martin Israel's feet in many a retreat, as I read the text of this volume I can easily imagine the somewhat staccato and authoritative cadences of the master's voice, always without notes, as if he in turn was 'listening inside' to the promptings of the Holy Spirit.

Actually the source of inspiration is less important than the content, so I ask the reader to assess what is written in the following pages in the light of truth. St John tells us to: 'Test the spirits, to see if they come from God... every spirit which acknowledges that Jesus the Christ has come in the flesh is from God.' (1 John 4.1-2) By this criterion Bess's book certainly passes the test of true prophecy. Indeed since Jesus is the Risen Lord, one should expect intimations of immortality from His discarnate followers. Certainly the proliferation of accounts of near-death experiences in our day bears witness to the reality of life beyond death, and of the sheer love and light that permeates the higher worlds. In the New Jerusalem: 'there is no need of sun or moon.... it is lit by the radiant glory of God, and the Lamb is a lighted torch for it.' (Rev.21.23).

A word on rebirth, which will be strange to many readers, as it's not a mainstream Christian doctrine. Martin's original vision in his early teens gave him intuitive knowledge 'of all his lives'. I told him once that my first hearing of Gregorian chant sent shivers down my spine, to which he replied: 'Ah, you've heard it before!' Bishop Montefiore believed belief in some form of rebirth: 'not incompatible with Christianity', citing Mark 9.13, of John the Baptist being Elijah, though not all agree with this interpretation. Hebrews 9.27: 'As men die only once...' seems to preclude further spells on earth, but its point is to emphasize Christ's 'one full, perfect and sufficient sacrifice for the sins of the whole world'. If I read Martin aright, this sacrifice avails for every incarnation on earth, including those re-sitting the exam many times as it were. In truth, the teaching is interesting but peripheral, for the 'whole duty of man' is to love God, and to love neighbour as self. Quite enough to keep us occupied.

Keith Denerley is a Vice President of the Churches' Fellowship for Psychical and Spiritual Studies

MARTIN ISRAEL:

A Short Biography

Martin Spencer Israel was born in Johannesburg, South Africa on 30th April 1927. During childhood, although he adhered to the liberal Judaism of his parents, Martin found himself strongly attracted to Christianity through the influence of the family's servants. His spiritual search was later to lead him to explore the Eastern religions, New Age phenomena and Quakerism, before he finally settled in the Anglican Church. His early childhood was far from happy and was blighted by sexual abuse from his father, an eminent eye surgeon. A lonely and introverted boy, he frequently found solace by escaping into a private world of music and mystical experience. The war years brought the tragic and shocking news that all of the family's Lithuanian relatives had been killed by the Nazis. Martin proved to be a brilliant scholar and went on to study medicine at the University of Witwatersrand, where he took first class honors. He came to Britain in 1951 to complete his postgraduate training and began his medical career as a house physician at the Hammersmith Hospital in London. This was followed by a period as a pathology registrar at the Royal Hospital, Wolverhampton. He spent his National Service in the Royal Army Medical Corps in Nigeria and Cyprus and then took up the post of Lecturer in Pathology at the Royal College of Surgeons in London. In 1963, he collaborated with a colleague: J. B. Walter, in the co-authoring of the standard textbook in Pathology.[1] He was promoted to Senior Lecturer in 1968. During adulthood Martin suffered severe bouts of depression, for which he sought the help of psychotherapy to good effect. He was called to ordination in 1974 and began his curacy at St Michael's Church, Cornhill. In 1983, he became Priest-in-Charge of Holy Trinity Church, Prince Consort Road, Kensington, where he remained for the next thirteen years. He was well known in Christian circles for his gift of spontaneous utterance, displaying an ability to speak at length without notes on spiritual subjects. He was also a prolific Christian author, leader of retreats, counselor and spiritual director to many. In early adulthood he discovered within himself a gift of healing and alongside his counseling skills; this became an integral part of his ministry. His psychic gifts and his interest in the afterlife led him to join the Churches' Fellowship for Psychical and Spiritual Studies, where he eventually became president from 1983 to 1998. He also held the presidency of the Guild of Health from 1983 to 1990 and was an adviser on exorcism to the Bishop of London. The all-encompassing nature of Martin's spiritual views proved attractive to many seekers. His central Christian message was based on the power of Jesus Christ to liberate the human soul into fullness of being.

Martin died on 23rd October 2007, aged 80, having suffered from Parkinson's Disease for a number of years.

1.

PASSING

To my friends and associates in the spirit - I send greetings and love.

My passing on 23rd October 2007 was essentially traumatic for me. I was sorely afraid. You may question this - I who lectured far and wide on the life hereafter. But it really makes little difference exactly what one believes. The exit from this earthly life and the process of being reborn into the next is very similar to a birth onto earthly soil, in that it is accompanied by pain. I had heard many accounts of near-death experiences during my priestly ministry, but I was completely unprepared for the wondrous shock of my own passage. As my body began to slip away, as it were, the things of the earth - the material - began to break up and to fade away and the things of the spirit began to assume greater form and reality. I immediately noticed a cessation of the physical pain and the general sense of gross ill health that had been my earthly lot for some eleven years. My soul took flight - - -. Some had described to me a rising or a floating upwards, but this was not my own experience at all. For me it was rather like stepping from one room to the next. A change of dimension as it were. There was a silence and the cacophony of hospital noise and chatter ceased abruptly. All was still and there was a pause - as if the whole universe held its breath on my account. Then a figure appeared or rather materialized before me. You will be surprised to learn that I recognized it to be the father who had so abused me during my early years on the earth. I could see at once that he had been transformed. As I looked at him I at once 'knew' him. I could see his past stretching back and I could clearly see the reason for his abuse of me. Therein came full forgiveness. We embraced and he went gently on. I have never seen him again. But with that embrace came a great release to my innermost soul.

For the duration of my illness, I had had much time for contemplation about my own death. Now the moment had arrived and I had at last passed through the veil that separates the finite from the infinite. To begin with, I found it difficult to sensibly absorb the fact that I had actually died and that I was about to experience all that I had previously held to be true concerning the afterlife. It was all mind-blowing stuff and a terrific shock as you might imagine. Indeed, my first reaction on arriving on the shores of eternity was to burst into copious tears. It was the type of inconsolable crying that reverberates through one's whole being and has its origin in the depths of one's soul. My distress was triggered by witnessing the disintegration of my etheric cord - the umbilical-like structure that connects soul to body during one's lifetime on the earth. This constituted a liberation from my ailing earthly body, but it also meant that I was now irrevocably separated from the earth and all whom I had known and loved there. I found myself in the midst of a place entirely strange and I had no conscious idea of what was likely to happen next. Of course there is a deliberate cloaking of all essential knowledge of the hereafter during one's earthly existence. This had been true in my own case, although I had discovered much in the course of my prayer and research. But like anyone else, I essentially saw: 'only puzzling reflections in a mirror'.[1] As I watched the earth plane disintegrate and disappear before my eyes, I found that I was surrounded by a type of impenetrable mist. I could neither see nor hear anything and it seemed that I was in the center of some sort of an etheric cloud. Temperature wise, I did not feel hot or cold - just pleasantly and securely warm and comfortable. Then, the mist slowly began to recede. Tears continued to flow unceasingly down my cheeks - indeed, there seemed no end to them - but in spite of this, I managed to make out a landscape of rolling, undulating hills. My first thought was that everything seemed markedly similar to the type of terrain that one might encounter anywhere upon the earth. I later realized with hindsight that this was a reception stage. The proffering of similar surroundings to that of the earth plane, given in order to lessen the initial shock of transition. I began to make out the forms of trees and I became aware of grass beneath my feet dotted with commonplace flowers - daisies and buttercups and suchlike. Although these were veritably ordinary in one sense, they differed from earthly flowers in that they emitted a transcendent glow which spoke of the glory of God. They also seemed to give forth a simultaneous shout of joy to all who would listen, proclaiming: 'I am! - and I was created by the great I AM!'

While I was absorbing all of this, I realized that I was not alone. Walking towards me across the grass came the figure of a small girl. She was simply dressed in a white cotton shift and had long shining brown hair caught back in an Alice band. Her countenance was intelligent, lit up by sparkling brown eyes and she had a glorious smile. She approached me boldly, seemingly quite unperturbed and unembarrassed by the sight of a grown man in tears. In her hands she carried a garland of flowers and she stood on tiptoe to place these around my neck. The scent from the flowers wafted about me, enfolding me in a gentle kiss of perfume. By this time, my tears were flowing so relentlessly that I fell to my knees in embarrassment and covered my face with my hands. Then I felt a gentle, tentative hand upon my shoulder and I chanced to take my hands away from my streaming face in order to properly look up at the girl. I noticed that in the center of her forehead glowed a bright light in the shape of a star of David. Similarly, in the area of her heart another light glowed which was circular in shape and seemed to stretch away endlessly into infinity. A third circle of light shone from her abdominal area. The girl was joined by a second person whom I at once recognized as Cloud - a spiritual 'buddy' of mine from my early years in the healing ministry. Cloud gently helped me to stand and then proceeded to enfold me in an enormous reassuring hug. He did not release me until my tears had begun to subside, whereupon he held me at arm's length and looked into my eyes. He did not speak with words, but proceeded to spill his thoughts into my mind, saying: 'Take your time - we have all of the time which is eternity. You are greatly loved here.' Then the girl slipped her hand into mine and began to lead me across the grass. There, a group of souls stood waiting. They greeted me and introduced themselves one by one, after which Cloud led me to stand in the center of the circle. I noticed that each soul was surrounded by an aura of green light. With one accord, these auric lights swept towards me and flowed into the center of my being, bringing a great sense of peace. Each member of the group also possessed a star-shaped light in the center of the forehead area. The lights blazed towards me in unison whereupon an answering light sprang into being in the center of my own forehead. At the same time, my mind became one with their minds. A great onrush of knowledge bubbled forth deep within me and I found that I was able to recall having lived through numerous lifetimes. As these identities flashed through my mind one by one, I was given a choice as to which physical persona I now wished to adopt. I chose to remain as I am, albeit a younger version of myself. (I now appear as a man in his early thirties - an era of my life that I particularly enjoyed while on the earth). Then a second light shone forth from the heart area of each group member and again these lights flowed towards me with one accord. As before, I became aware of the formation of an answering light within my own heart area. These lights then mingled and I became of one heart with the group. With this union of heart, I experienced unconditional love, acceptance and a deep sense of belonging. It is difficult to convey in words the sheer depth and intensity of this whole experience. But, suffice it to say, it became abundantly clear that we lead comparatively separate and lonely existences while we are on the earth. Except, of course, when we form a close relationship with another kindred spirit. As I stood united to the group by mind and by heart, I noticed that within this state of union, nothing was lost of our individual identities, despite the sense of complete oneness with the group. Then a third light appeared within the abdominal area of each member of the group. These flowed towards me and I again experienced the ignition of an answering light in my own abdomen. I then found myself united by this light to each soul. This place of union seemed to consist of a deep emotional bond.

And so, there I stood, in the midst of the group, linked by a threefold circle of lights. I peeked a look at this point and saw that each person had their eyes closed. I was intensely curious of course and I desperately wished to say something and to ask questions, but at this moment, it was clear that I was not being invited to do so. Then, within this state of union, we began to ascend upwards. The vast misty plane of rolling hills began to disappear beneath us and there was a sense of rapid traveling - a flashing past of shapes, forms and colors. We moved along what appeared to be countless tunnels of light and I saw glimpses of wonders that are indescribable in earthly terms. After what seemed to be a long period of time, we finally reached a vast cavern which was filled with intense white light. I opened my eyes fully and at once became aware of a complete lack of physical impairment. Especially noticeable was the sense of mobility in my limbs. Having spent such a long period confined to a wheelchair and capable of very little movement, this constituted a great liberation as you might imagine. I also noticed that my sight was restored to complete clarity and lucidity and that I was able to hear with a sharpness that I had not enjoyed for many long years. I glanced down at my body and I discovered that my limbs were straight and perfectly formed. I had returned to the physical state of a man in the prime of his life. I looked around at the group and saw that upon each face was a broad smile and, in some cases tears. Then, a member of the group walked towards me. His face was ancient yet essentially ageless and his eyes danced and shone with a youthful vitality. I wondered momentarily if this was the Christ, such was his demeanor of purity and love. Yet this was not the Savior - this was an ancient soul - an echelon of light whose name is Maccabee. He drew me into a warm embrace - as a father might greet a beloved child who has been long away. Then he spoke a name that flashed through my being like a streak of lightening. This was not the name by which I had been known upon the earth. This was my spiritual name - the name by which I am known on this side of life - the name which was engraved upon my heart by God at the beginning of time.

Then, within the cavern of light, I became completely united with these souls to whom I belong in Christ - the group known collectively as AVESHIDA. Our name, roughly translated, means 'praise and peace' and we number sixteen in all. How much time all of this took I cannot say, for I have learned that time on this side of life is a completely different concept altogether. Incidentally, I had experienced the intriguing phenomenon of time versus eternity on the earth when, after having been in a state of deep prayer for some while, I would return to discover that an inordinate amount of time had elapsed. When it seemed that I had been in prayer for a period of around ten minutes, I would glance with astonishment at my timepiece to discover that several hours had gone by. Of course I had the privilege of giving in to this state more liberally during my time as an invalid. For no one minded when I appeared to doze off indiscriminately into what was actually a state of deep prayer. The friends who visited me during this time were thankfully very tolerant of this.

Then, as a group, we sat cross-legged in a circle and

various exchanges began to take place. This was not mere aimless chatter, but a deep exchange of the light of meeting. A 'crossfire' of light began. As this happened, I received details about each soul, including knowledge of their previous incarnations. This was a lot to take on board all at once, but I was beginning to discover that the longer I spent in the rarified atmosphere of the lighted cavern, the more receptive I was becoming to all that was happening to me. The lights within each person's heart area linked with the light in my own heart and there occurred a deep exchange of love. As each member of the group poured their love towards me, an answering flow of love traveled back in kind from my own heart. For this was not an initial meeting with these souls. I was beginning to realize that I had spent many lifetimes in their company, within varying earthly situations and modes of relatedness. During the linking of heart to heart, the remembrance of all of these connections was revealed to me. My exchange with the group brought about the re-establishment of the deep bond of indefinable, immeasurable love with these souls. I was beginning to discover in the deepest and fullest sense that: 'love is built to last forever'.[2]

2.

COMING HOME

The crossfire of light culminated in a complete state of union between myself and the group. Then a channel of pure energy manifested itself in our midst, in the center of which appeared an angel. His face was passive and beautiful and his eyes were like pools of blue. In his hands he carried a folded garment. Maccabee walked towards him with eyes cast downwards - one could not look directly into the angel's face for too long due to the intensity of his light. After handing the garment to Maccabee, the angel turned his gaze to me. This caused me to feel somewhat vulnerable - there had been so much to take on board all at once and my mind suddenly began to rebel with an overload of new concepts and information. But at last I did look up into his face - it would have been rude not to. And oh - to try to describe what I saw. Within those wonderful eyes was manifested the pure unadulterated love of God. Then two smaller angelic presences appeared within the lighted shaft of energy. They flew upwards and grasped the edges of the folded cloth, shaking it out to its full length. It was revealed to be a hooded robe, the colors of which brought to my mind the remembrance of springtime. Then the angels flew above me and gently placed the robe over my head. As it fell about my person there came a sudden burst of ethereal music. I was momentarily transported back to a time during my youth when I had once been lifted up into Paradise while listening to beautiful music. But at this moment of receiving my robe, I was now in Paradise, rather than glimpsing it from afar. As the robe embraced my person, I was filled with the deep joy of coming home and of essential belonging.

Then all three angels disappeared into the shaft of lighted energy and I was once again alone with the group AVESHIDA. I was invited to stand within the perimeter of the circle, whereupon all of our lights became fused - mind to mind, heart to heart, abdomen to abdomen. Once we were linked in this threefold way, the lights began to spin through our beings, forming three rings. The cavern then began to disappear beneath us and we traveled into a vast open space of complete nothingness. All around us was a void - formless and endless, containing no substance or structure. Within the nothingness was pure, undiluted love. I found myself relaxing fully for the first time since my passing. It felt that I was encountering that which I had sought so relentlessly in prayer during my lifetime on the earth - the all-pervading Spirit of God. Endless, formless, limitless and eternal. Within the void I received the sense of becoming fully 'real'. I came to the realization that while on the earth we are like actors on a stage set of existence and that all perceived 'reality' around us is essentially flimsy.

In the midst of the void, we entered a place of intense white light. I could see nothing except for a blinding whiteness, pure as a magnesium flare. Then we seemed to be pulled forwards into the center of an eye and there was a sense of falling as if from a great height, yet I was not afraid for I remained linked to the group by the three rings of kinetic energy. I was also surrounded by the caressing gentleness of pure love contained within the void. The whiteness of the light eventually exploded into a blaze of blue and green and we landed on a surface that was soft and springy. As my vision cleared, I saw before us a large building constructed of marble pillars. The building stood within cultivated gardens of hedgerows, rose blooms, lawns, streams and shining ponds upon which sailed brightly colored water birds. The sky was blue, edged with a soft pink horizon. There was the scent of roses everywhere. I immediately recognized it to be a place of healing. There was a 'vibration' in the surrounding ether that was reminiscent of my ministry of healing on the earth. Down the steps of the building came a figure wearing white robes. The person possessed a similar countenance to Maccabee and I knew that we were in the presence of another ancient soul. I could not immediately tell if the person was male or female but such delineation did not seem to matter, so great was the concept of integration. The face was surrounded by an aura of pure white and the eyes were blue-green, containing an element which invited a gratifying sense of both safety and surrender. One felt drawn into the depths of the eyes by the force of love and once one allowed this to happen, nothing else seemed important. As we entered the building I saw that the interior was similar to a hospital of sorts. There were long vast corridors and the entrances of the rooms were door-less and bathed in bright white light. We eventually came to a halt outside one of the rooms and I was invited to enter. Inside was an orb surrounded by three spinning rings of light. As I entered the room, I assumed a weightlessness that induced a sensation of being cradled in the softest of duck down. The being of light gently guided me into a horizontal position several feet from the floor. There seemed nothing else to do but to relax and at all times I felt completely safe, secure and unthreatened. The being of light then moved the orb so that it enclosed the top part of my head. It felt similar to wearing a type of helmet but it caused no sense of claustrophobia since it was completely transparent. Then I began to experience continuous flashbacks of my most recent lifetime on the earth, with all of its joys and sorrows. How long this continued I do not know, for, as I have already said, the concept of time within eternity is completely nebulous and unquantifiable. Once the memories were completely played out (the last memory being the moment of my birth) I remained within a state of rest for a very long period. I was not aware of much while I was in this state. My body and mind were completely still and all of the struggle, striving and vicissitudes of my life on the earth plane melted cleanly away. At intervals, I experienced a sense of visiting the earth - the places, people and situations that had been important to me. As I encountered these, I blessed them and then moved on. The whole process bore a similarity to the concept of moving to a new abode - the checking out of one's former dwelling place to make sure beforehand that everything is shipshape and in order. Eventually I reached a sense of being completely at peace with the earth and with all whom I had known there.

After this time of consolidation and renewal, I experienced a meeting with Our Savior and His Blessed Mother. The Christ appeared enshrouded in light and emanating pure love. He was very much as our pictures on the earth depict. Bearded with long flowing auburn hair which waved and curled to just below shoulder length. He wore a long simple robe. Nothing grand at all. I could see the wounds in His hands and in His feet. Through His robe the wound in His side was also visible. The Holy Mother stood beside Him. She was dark haired with intense blue eyes and remained watchful and quiet. The disciple John stood a few steps behind Our Lord - a sandy haired youth with a pure face. A circle of white doves surrounded by rainbow auras fluttered overhead and angelic beings stood on guard around the three figures. The angels were extremely large - around three meters in height. They wore chain mail and were surrounded in a golden light. You could clearly see their 'given-ness' to God. It was something about the way their eyes spoke of God. How did I feel at this point? As I stood before the Christ - the One Whom I had worshiped for the greater part of my earthly life? Well, it was like 'coming home' in a very big way - like the fitting of the last piece of a jigsaw. A lot of what Christ said to me was private, between myself and Him alone and these things I will treasure in the secrecy of my own heart forever more. But the most wonderful moment of all was when He spoke one particular word - my name. How that word resounded within my heart. To hear Him - the Holiest of all Holies speaking my name. If I was ever in any doubt that I was loved at all by God, these doubts were dispelled entirely at that most precious of moments. Any suffering that I had undergone. Any trial. Any sin that I had committed during my earthly existence (and we all do - I was not perfect). Everything was made whole in the utterance of my name by the Holiest of all Holies.

Then the gentle Mother of Christ stepped forward and embraced me, saying: 'Well done, O good and faithful servant.' Her smile seemed to anoint my innermost soul. She was enshrouded in golden light and within her solar plexus area I could clearly see a second aura of light in the shape of an unborn child - the infant Christ. It is difficult for me to adequately convey the impact of all of this and to describe the sheer wonder of it. Except to say that everything within me cried in unison: 'Glory, glory, GLORY!' The Holy Mother wore a golden cloak, which reflected a myriad of eddying lights and contained within the cloak were the burdens that she carries on behalf of humankind. Her cloak was somehow a part of her own aura and thus it became clear to me that she directly shares the agony of the world. I was also shown that from the moment of the Annunciation - the time of the receiving of the angel's message, followed by her reply: 'may it be as you have said,'[1] - she, the holiest of all women, became no longer human, but divine. She was plucked as a girl, from humankind, for the greatest of all vocations and at that moment in time she was rendered a divine being. She bore in her womb the Author of all that is and all that shall be. She left the human race at the moment of her unconditional assent and became the future Queen of Heaven. For she was and is the greatest of all mothers. In meeting her in this way, I felt as if a great wound within my own soul was finally healed. This encounter with the holiest of all mothers caused the pain of my childhood to be miraculously unraveled and rewoven into a perfect cloth. The very fact that the threads that made up this cloth had once added up to much pain, meant that the rewoven picture, in some mysterious way, was altogether more perfect and more beautiful because it had been wrought through pain. I was reminded momentarily of the atrocity of the Cross. I am not being sacrilegious here in comparing my own lot as an abused child with Christ's own suffering, for His death on the Cross encompassed all of the pain of humankind. In this way, my own pain and the pain of all of the abused was nailed there with Him as He suffered. What came to me during the embrace of the Holy Mother was the word: 'resurrection'. The resurrection of one small frightened abused boy. The boy who had lived in anguish within me since those early traumatic years. A boy in tears. A boy crying for the mother who never came. The mother who had turned away from her own son's suffering simply because it would not be seemly or tasteful to broadcast the presence of such abuse within her perfect household. But whose inner anguish and turmoil about the situation drove her to the edge of an emotional precipice.

My emotion overtakes me as I speak of this to you and I once again give heartfelt thanks for the wondrous healing at this deep level that I received in entirety from the Queen of all women.

After this encounter, my soul was taken from glory to glory and I saw and experienced things beyond imagination and thought and telling which are not possible to convey in earthly terms. Over these things I must cast a veil.

3.

THE GROUP SOUL

What is the life of eternity like? I will endeavor to answer the questions that would spring to my own mind. With the exception of two of our members, all of our group live fairly close to each other on the Seventh Level of existence. We are not 'joined at the hip', to coin a modern phrase. We all have our own habitations, except for those members whose soul is twinned with another. As individuals and as a group we are constantly evolving. The individuals that we are now are not what we have always been, but basically contain the same elements. In outward appearance each member of AVESHIDA has chosen to reflect their last existence on the earth.

As a group we travel frequently to other spheres and our main purpose is the rescue of lost souls who are trapped in the lower regions. While carrying out this work our collective light is so bright that no darkness can overcome it. There is great joy in seeing a lost soul freed and healed. My work was similar to this of course while I was on the earth, but it is so much more rewarding to carry it out here collectively as a member of a group soul.

When we are together, the group is completely cohesive and all are in tune one with another. This affords relief after the relative experience of aloneness on the earth plane. To be able to abandon oneself to a group and to exist alongside others in total harmony is a wonderful thing indeed. The group members never disagree or squabble at all because of the fact that we are completely of one mind and one heart.

Those for whom we pray on the earth become enfolded, surrounded and permeated by our waves of love. But although we may support individuals on the earth by protecting them with impenetrable light, we are never allowed to directly intervene in any situation at all. The reason for this is free will. Every individual life situation on the earth must be permitted to play itself out to its allotted conclusion and we are not allowed to alter a specific course of events in any sense.

On this side of being the relationships between souls directly mirrors their past associations on the earth. In the general sense, the human race can be said to be a co-reacting organism within which individual souls respond sympathetically one with another. During earthly existence, one may not be consciously aware of such relatedness, but in fact there exists a whole myriad of hidden eternal connections with others. An example of one such associative link is the dualistic state known as the duo-soul. In such cases the soul has an alter ego and each is entirely simpatico with the other. Such souls orbit around each other in the spiritual sense like two planets in the same gravitational field. They are not identical but parallel. Their existence is expressed as a type of dance of souls and there is great beauty in the interaction. Such souls will always be together ultimately, but for the purpose of earthly incarnation they initially exist alone and are usually incarnated together on the earth into differing modes of existence. From the moment of birth each constantly strives to locate the other and they will have no rest until their partner is found. Once this happens a strong allegiance is formed, the meaning of which may sometimes not be fully realized until both reach this side of being. Colloquially speaking they can be termed as 'soul mates' or 'kindred spirits'. They will never experience true wholeness until they are reunited. Once this takes place they quite literally 'light up' and begin to become their true selves. Earthly existence and heavenly existence may overlap and one may eventually pass on before the other. But this does not break the link. After a short and intensely painful break they are normally able to commune and communicate through the curtain that separates earthly existence from heavenly existence. A comparable state of relatedness is that of the twinned soul. This consists of two souls who are completely identical to each other at the level of the spirit and totally in harmony. Yet another type of soul interaction is that of compatibles - souls who weave in and out of each another as one, but exist separately. Translating all of these concepts from the realm of eternity to the level of the finite is very difficult, as the consciousness expands greatly when one arrives here and suddenly everything becomes clear. Suffice it to say that all relationships of love begin on the earth and then continue on here. Relationships of the aforementioned types cannot actually begin here on this side of being. I have seen this very clearly.

The group soul essentially comprises a circle of light which contains interconnecting minds and hearts in continuous communication with one another. Nothing is hidden on this side of being and as a group we share everything, both good and bad, about ourselves. By 'bad' I mean the darkness that is in us all - that which is still being redeemed until such time as we reach the ultimate place of absorption into God's light and love. There is also a connecting ring of love adjacent to the ring of light and a ring of divine energy. The greatest joy on this side of being is communion with other souls and this is especially the case if one previously lived alone. There is great joy in the knowledge that one will never be alone again and that henceforward one will always be supported and upheld.

The names of my counterparts within the group AVESHIDA are: Cloud, Marylu, Mabel, Ian, Florence, Frances, Helen, Gérard, Geoffrey, William, Sulo, Cedric, Edgar, Leung and Maccabee. I knew AVESHIDA in the spiritual sense during my time on the earth and I had also previously known some of the members individually on the physical plane. When I first passed over it was a great thrill to meet up with old friends from long ago and there was many a grand reunion.

Regarding the individual group members of AVESHIDA, Marylu is the young girl who welcomed me with the garland of flowers after my passing. She appears outwardly as a child, but in fact she is a very old and exalted soul. She will continue to exist in a state of childhood throughout eternity. She helps AVESHIDA especially when our work involves the souls of children who have passed over in traumatic circumstances - a violent death or some suchlike. Marylu is responsible for greeting such souls in the first instance. She has the necessary gentle touch and is able to gain their confidence. Everyone on the earth is familiar with cases when a child is taken at too young an age, causing much distress to all concerned. Marylu has had many such incarnations as a child during which she subsequently died in childhood. She does not live with the group, but dwells on the plane of eternal childhood and is looked after there. This is a wondrous, beautiful place of which I will give more details later.

Mabel is a large, comforting, motherly soul who took me firmly under her wing when I first arrived here. This was my first introduction to mothering, having never experienced anything of this sort as a child during my earthly life. It was necessary because, due to my sensitivity, I found the very act of passing over intensely painful in the emotional sense and a gross bereavement in itself. I mourned the loss of all that I had known on the earth - even my incapacitated state. It was what I had become accustomed to and to suddenly be free of all of that was terribly traumatic. You may well ask how one could possibly become attached to a useless body and a failing mind. The truth is that one tends to cling to what is familiar, good or bad, and my days as an invalid had been filled with dependence. I had become converted; as it were;

to the life of a dependent. So when I first arrived here, Mabel generously gave of her unbounded love and care.

Ian is Mabel's partner. They are twinned souls and each complements the other. Latterly, on the earth, they were man and wife, but they 'go back a long way' as they say. They work together and exist together in every way. They will never be separated again and will never return to the earth plane.

If Mabel played the role of surrogate mother when I first arrived here, then Cloud was my spiritual father and to some extent he still fulfils that role for me. Cloud, during his last incarnation, was a North American Indian. We are allowed to choose our external embodiment and outer form from that which was our favorite incarnation on the earth. In Cloud's case, this was his life latterly in North America, when he was martyred for his faith and belief in Christ. He is a very old soul and he will never be incarnated again on the earth. His work now is entirely spiritual. Since my passing we have spent a lot of time in each other's company and he has taught me a lot.

Cedric and Edgar existed as a gay couple on the earth and were at the receiving end of much bigotry during the era in which they lived. They are twinned souls and were partners on the earth at a time when homosexuality was a complete anathema and not accepted at all. And indeed is still not among the more unenlightened, but don't get me started on that at this stage. On the earth they were essentially ordinary men - but extraordinary - due to all that they suffered vicariously for the gay community. They are a very important element in the group and they bring much love and sanity with their clear thinking and humor. I love them both dearly and they too have helped me a lot.

I knew Geoffrey during my last incarnation and he was a great friend to me during a specific period of my life, of which I will give details elsewhere. It is always a surprise to meet up with old friends again even though one has always known that this will be the case.

I also knew Gérard while I was on the earth. Latterly he was a Frenchman and he showed great bravery in his work in the Resistance movement during World War Two. He did not die in this capacity but went on to live to a very great age. He became a real prayer warrior in later life, for which his earlier battles against the powers of darkness had equipped him. He has continued with this work latterly on the spiritual plane.

I knew Helen and Frances during my early ministry on the earth. They were Christian sensitives and were skilled in the art of telepathy. From this relationship evolved the epistle written by Helen in collaboration with Frances after the latter's passing.[1] This is a wonderful work which has served to contribute much to the understanding of those interested in the life hereafter. In the general sense, love is the key to all telepathic communication - the linking of minds and hearts. It is love that creates the bridge between the earth and the world to come. In fact love is the basis of everything - I cannot stress this enough.

Lovely, gentle Florence was a servant in my household during the loveless time of my boyhood which so damaged me emotionally. She is a beautiful soul and was responsible for leading me to Christ in the first instance. I didn't realize at that time how important she was to be in my life and what a great soul she was. I was delighted to see her smiling face greeting me when I was enfolded into the group on my arrival here.

Leung was latterly from Eastern shores - China to be exact - where he worked tirelessly as a Christian evangelist and succeeded in winning many souls for the Kingdom of God.

Maccabee is the oldest soul among us and is rare indeed. As Marylu is youthful, so he is old. He has a very refined consciousness and he travels extensively throughout the spheres. During his last incarnation he was a desert monk who fought against the powers of darkness in complete solitude. He has great depths and I am learning a lot from him. He is complicated and there is much more to him than meets the eye. He goes back a very long way and has appeared in various forms, but basically he has always been the same. He is one of the higher echelons of light and as such he does not live on our plane but dwells much further on in the light. He has made a specific choice to return in order to assist us in our work.

William is a very emotionally wounded soul and he uses this woundedness to help those who are in need. He is perpetually broken and through his spiritual suffering others are able to be reached who could not otherwise be reached. He appears to be a somewhat somber character initially, but nothing could be further from the truth. He can be as gay and frivolous as Marylu at times. But at the same time he carries a lot and exists as a spiritual vessel. He has the ability to filter distress from the souls we encounter in the lower regions and he holds this pain within himself until he is able to disperse and offload it into the light. He does wonderful work. He has made the choice to remain broken and wounded until the end of time in order to help others.

Sulo was latterly a Ugandan who suffered terrible persecution on the earth. Like Cloud he was martyred for his faith in Christ. He died a cruel death and, as with William, he continues to suffer emotional agony on behalf of others. There is great pain within him and he carries a lot. Only at the end of time will William and Sulo be healed. For the moment their state of perpetual woundedness is their spiritual vocation on this side of being. I myself had a similar calling while on the earth and I was a wounded channel for healing as such.

So that completes our number. As you can see, our individual characters are as varied as the flowers in the field. As a group, AVESHIDA is a body of complementing parts with all sorts of differing essential elements which make up the whole. This is what St Paul meant when he spoke of the parts of a body and each having its own function.[2] Every facet and nuance that we can possibly encounter in our healing work is represented within the group and in this way we are able to reach those who need to be reached. All of our disparate elements go together to make one cohesive body.

In general my life here is the culmination of everything I have ever dreamed of and hoped for. I am continually excited and filled with the greatest of joy by the wonder of it all. As I have mentioned, we exist on the Seventh Level of being - a place of light that is very near to the New Jerusalem. There are many higher souls here. It is a place that is completely enclosed in light, peace and beauty. God's creativity has run riot here! There are mountain ranges on every side and snow falls on the highest peaks. The sky is always blue and there is no inclement weather. Flowers abound of every variety and type. Flowers that do not die or wither. The horticultural experts among you would indeed be in seventh heaven! There are trees too. Majestic trees that are alive with the light of God. Ashes and oaks, pines, aspens and willows - all varieties. There are forests and woodlands, streams and waterfalls. We also have animals. Those with favored pets on the earth are able to be reunited with them as they so wish. A case in point is Cloud - who has with him a beloved horse from the time of his last existence on the earth. The horse's name is 'Footprint' and I see them together morning by morning, galloping along the shore.

As you can see, there are animals in the heavenly realms and they too have their own sphere and ladder of progress into the light of God. As such there are 'greater' and 'lesser' animal souls. Animals go through a similar journey of passing through a series of progressive spheres, but it is very much simpler in their case. When they reach a certain point they have the choice of returning to their former owners on this side of being when a positive bond of love has been present. Several members of AVESHIDA have been reunited with loved animals following their passing. In my own case, I had had little experience of this during my earthly life. The barren emotional climate of my childhood and my busy adult life had precluded this. Shortly after my passing the group decided that it would be beneficial for my healing process to have the companionship of an animal. As many earthly animal lovers know, those who are grossly wounded in the emotional sense are often helped by relating to a pet, when other relationships prove difficult. Thus, when I reached this side of being, my fellow members of AVESHIDA presented me with a small kitten - also recently passed over. Maccabee first came up with the idea and, not wishing to hurt his feelings, I decided to go along with it as best as I could. However, despite my initial misgivings, I took to the relationship like a proverbial duck to water. The kitten is a pretty little thing and I named him 'Blue', as one of the first things I noticed about him was that he has a faint bluish tinge to his fur. He is a very advanced animal soul and he will not return again to the earth. He will continue with AVESHIDA when we eventually travel on into the light of God. As regards his past history, he was severely mistreated on the earth, was consequently very wounded in the area of trust and had many fears. When he first arrived, his appearance was somewhat scrawny and ill-kempt. I was informed of the details of the past cruelties he had endured and how he had died. I will not go into detail about the indignities he went through at the hands of human beings who acted in a less than human manner towards him. It is all too horrible to convey and it upsets me to even think about it. Once he had a name, the ice seemed proverbially broken and we began to exist together in an altogether companionable way. He got up to various antics and from the start he had the ability to make me smile. As time went on I noticed that he began to appear less scrawny and that his fur became smooth and shining. He began to follow me everywhere, padding along on his tiny paws. After a while, I took pity on him and habitually started scooping him up whenever I went anywhere. Thus, he took up almost permanent residence in a large pocket of my robes. The love and affection that he gave me from the start was constant and unconditional, despite the fact that initially my company must have been a lonely business for him. But as time went on my own reserve began to melt and now I cannot imagine ever being without him. Both of us were essentially in need of love and we continue to bring healing to each other in this way. Mabel tells me that, since my arrival here, I am 'opening like a flower in the light of God's healing love'.

My own dwelling place on the Seventh Level is high upon a cliff. It is a windswept place and a charming abode. It is quite near to a woodland and has a garden filled with glorious flowers. I look out across the sea and each morning I walk along the shore and give thanks that my incapacity is no more. Our Lord tells us in the gospel of St John: 'There are many dwelling-places in my Father's house.'[3] This is indeed the case. The Seventh Level is the highest level of existence and prior to this there are six gradients of light. Level One is the lowest level and is the reception stage through which all souls pass initially. This first level is essentially one of assessment, review and healing and as such, it is a benign area and a neutral zone. Here, there is much surrounding cloud which creates a perpetual sense of haziness. It is a level which is purely functional and no one lives here permanently. The higher echelons of light, of which Maccabee is one, come and go in ministry. Reunions also take place and souls may travel in and out to greet their loved ones. Here on the Seventh Level there are wonderful views and vistas everywhere which are very edifying. Rivers flow into unending oceans and the oceans are filled, not with water and salt, but with the gold of God's enduring love and charity. The angels sing all of the time around the throne of God and there is a pathway encrusted with diamonds that leads through the foothills to the Heavenly Jerusalem.

Communication on this side of being is largely telepathic and one is also able to move from place to place at will. When we meet another soul, the knowledge of all there is to know about them comes in a flash and a type of 'knowing'. Just by being in the presence of another soul, one is immediately able to see all of their past and all of their previous experiences. But one does have control over such perception. One can choose to 'let it in' or not so to speak. There is also complete transparency of thought and feeling. I must admit that I found this aspect difficult at first. I still do to a certain extent because of my natural predisposition to privacy, caused by the pain of my upbringing in my last incarnation. When one first passes over, one is in a very sensitive state. Consider how one would feel if one's skin was peeled off and one was red and raw. One immediately has to learn to cope with the revelation that absolutely everyone can see you exactly as you are and the lack of privacy this brings. We do not have the luxury of solitude here, but, as I have said, each of us does have a private place to which we can retreat in order to 'recharge' as it were. This was something that I found especially welcome at the beginning.

There are many aspects of the life of eternity that are inevitably 'lost in translation'. The reason for this, as I have said before, is that the earthly finite mind does not have the capability to encompass the entirety of the infinite life. There is a deliberate cloaking of full understanding during earthly existence. If we were able to achieve complete comprehension during our incarnate life, our period of earthly testing would not be real and valid at all. As that wonderful passage in St Paul's letter to the Corinthians reminds us: 'My knowledge now is partial; then it will be whole, like God's knowledge of me.'[4] I myself am not as I was and I now have a freedom that I could never previously have perceived would be possible. I am expanded and actualized. This is quite a complicated state of affairs about which, again, I am unable to elaborate in earthly terms. But once one reaches the higher levels on this side of being, all becomes clear and understanding is complete. The mind expands greatly as one gradually moves further forward. But the conscious mind is extremely limited and is geared only to the permutations of the physical world.

Everyone on this side of being exists upon differing planes of realization and growth. Everyone is absorbed into as much light and truth as they can bear. The journey into the light of God is essentially an act of becoming. God, the Father of all, is an energy and a force of love dwelling within each human heart. He is also a Trinitarian Being. On this side of being there is a golden light transfusing everything and within this light is a Heart which is the source of everything that exists. Christ - the One who came to earth to save us all - dwells in the center entirely.

As part of our existence on the Seventh Level, we have access to divine power. At the very center of our sphere is the beating Heart of God. Tributaries run from it - which are rivers of light. These are rather akin to 'veins' and consist of vast channels which course along in a type of network of rivers throughout the sphere. Hovering above the channels are diaphanous angels who form a kind of intricate web - a gossamer type of substance. At intervals along the rivers are vast waterfalls of tumbling golden water. These run into deep pools which are imbued with divine power. When we bathe in this water or drink from it, we are instilled with power from on high. While this power lasts we have the ability to heal, forgive and minister in the Name of Christ. This enables and empowers us to carry out our work. As such we are God's agents, as it were, on this side of being. Gradually, gradually we are building up to a point where we are so infused with the light and power of God, that we will become Christified. This will happen in the twinkling of an eye, in a trice and in a moment. It is then that we will journey on towards mysteries that are beyond telling and imagination and beyond speech and thought. But for the present, our work is here on the Seventh Level and the time of our moving onward is known only to Almighty God.

Existence in a group soul is comparable to the aspect of earthly experience which is generally spent within the bounds and protection of one group or another. As the Scriptures tell us: 'God gives the lonely a home to live in,'[5] and: 'It is not good for the man to be alone.'[6] So it is on the greater side of being. In my own case, my family on the earth was essentially dysfunctional and I had no sense of belonging at all. But this is not always the case, thank God. There are many wonderfully cohesive families on the earth plane which serve as an example to us all. In such cases, the individual family members create such a bond of love with one another during their earthly lives, that their only wish is to continue within their family group in the life hereafter and indeed they will be able to do so. A delightful reunion will take place on their passing and they will find that their familial devotion has survived the bounds of death. There are also other types of group on this side of existence that pertain to interests, talents and persuasions of various types. Science for example. For research continues in the greater life. Solutions to various medical problems on the earth plane are constantly sought over here and all inspiration in the field of medical research on the earth plane originates on this side of life. However, the solutions reached must ultimately come about on the earth plane itself. For the earth is evolving, telling its own story and creating its own collective memory as it were. It would be easy for advanced souls on this side of being to 'feed' and convey various solutions to one problem or another on the earth. But that would be doing a great disservice to all concerned and would take away the whole essence of free will. No - the future of the earth is completely in the hands of humankind and as such, it is arriving at its own conclusions. We, on this side of being, may help by observing and protecting with our prayers, but we must not interfere in any sense. The earth is in charge of its own destiny both individually and collectively. Every situation on the earth must be allowed to play itself out to its own conclusion.

The source of all things is God Himself and all creativity has its origin within the Divine and is essentially inspired. God is Creator and we are His cohorts. We thus allow His creativity to work through us. The divine spark within our souls, when allowed free expression, gives rise to all manner of creative possibilities. But each creative work - each project; as it were; bears the stamp of the individual through whom the divine inspiration flows at any one time. We are all therefore in cohesive cooperation with the Divine. We are co-creators of the wondrous tapestry of artistic expression while on the earth. We are not 'puppets' in any sense, but when we allow the flow of God's love and energy to rise unimpeded within our innermost souls, creative expression is endless and the possibilities are infinitely glorious. And so it is over here. Those, for instance, who have excelled in the field of music while on earth, may progress to a group over here where they will have the opportunity to rise to even greater heights in this area. I have visited such groups since my passing. Oh - what glory - I cannot tell you. All of the arts, every aspect and facet you could think of is represented over here. Of course, as I have said previously, our group AVESHIDA has its own purpose of healing and redemption. This is a work which began for me while on the earth with my training in the medical field and continued latterly with the doctoring of souls. The former helped greatly when approaching the latter. It was a good grounding so to speak. Each member of AVESHIDA is gifted in a different way and each has something unique and special to contribute to the whole.

There are bands of light here. In the case of a group like AVESHIDA, the bands connecting us all resonate at the same frequency. I am sure that you have probably experienced something of this sort in your own lives. For instance, following an initial meeting, one might afterwards say: 'I felt on the same wavelength' as this person or that person. The opposite is also true of course. With some people one does not resonate at all and the encounter is disastrous from the start. This is the beginning of the process of psychic perception which will be experienced at greater depth in the life beyond death.

As soon as one reaches this side of being, the differentiating factor which stands out most obviously is the accentuation of one's powers of communication. There is an immediate heightening of unity between oneself and all other souls, which is beyond comparison to the isolation that we commonly experience during our mortal lives. Incidentally, this sort of communication would be possible on the earth if we but allowed ourselves full openness to all of our latent faculties. Most of us are, in fact, accessing only a very small portion of our abilities. We are closed to so much and we do not give ourselves the opportunity to improve on this state of affairs at all. We allow ourselves to become sidetracked by the sheer busy distractedness and relentlessness of our mortal existence. Our focus tends to be primarily upon all that is outside of us, and this trend of emphasis denies the possibility of reaping the rich harvest that lies untapped within most souls.

You may wonder what happens after the Seventh Level and how everything continues, as one journeys onward into the greater reaches of light? Well, AVESHIDA will remain together as a group. This we have been told. But once we continue onward, we will then be out of reach of the earth plane. We will be traveling towards even greater mysteries. We catch glimpses of this already - to prepare us so to speak. It will be a wondrous thing.

As previously mentioned, the work of AVESHIDA is mainly carried out in the lower regions. We go down as a group to carry out rescue work among the lost. A great battle rages on this side of being, which mirrors the struggle that you yourselves undergo on the earth. This is a battle that will continue until the end of time. But life here is not all work - we have many pleasures to enjoy as well and there is much beauty everywhere. The lack of aloneness is a great bonus - one is conjoined to other souls and love flows through each heart. Within AVESHIDA we are moving towards Christification and this is being wrought by sacrifice. We have each had many lives and all of us have endured the cross in one form or another. Our collective mind has the ability to operate as one when we are together as a group. We have many permutations and many characteristics that we do not possess when we are alone. AVESHIDA have always been together as a group, but not as the individuals that we are now. Since the beginning of time, we have been evolving. But as I have said already, our outward appearances now reflect our last incarnations on the earth.

As a group we meet together on a regular basis for collective prayer within the light of God. In this way, we are able to 'top up' our spiritual energies which then enables us to continue with the work appointed to us. At the start of any prayer session, we form a circle - sitting, or standing. Then, individually, we begin to pray and to focus inwardly. During this process, a light forms within each of our hearts which slowly expands until the whole of the chest area is imbued with that light. This light then links up with the light of the person on either side of us. This process happens collectively so that the whole group is at once linked by a band of light - heart joining heart. Then, the same process is repeated, but this time in the area of our minds. Thus, a light comes into being within each of our minds, which is visible in the forehead area. These lights then expand and flow outwards to link with those on either side of us. Again this happens collectively so that the whole group is linked mind to mind by a band of light at exactly the same moment. Then a light forms within each of our abdominal areas, and again, these expand and link with the lights of those on either side of us. We are thus joined in the abdominal area by a band of light. And so, at this point, we are united by three rings of light - one running through in the heart area, one through the head area and one through the abdominal area. An angel is present during our prayer sessions and he stands in the middle of the circle. Within his heart a star of light is visible and the points of this star flow out to connect with each of our hearts.

Once we are thoroughly focused upon our collective prayer, the circles of light begin to spin rapidly and to change color, flashing through the whole range of the spectrum. The angel's star also changes color in a similar way. At this point, we are completely one in soul and are no longer individuals. We have become one unit entirely. Then we are lifted up from the Seventh Level on a wave of energy and we travel directly into the light of God. During such a journey, we experience wonders that are beyond the description of the human mind. These are the wonders of God. We are imbued with love and with light. We travel through the greater reaches of light and we see and perceive things which cannot be described in words. Things that are of God.

When we return to the Seventh Level, we are on fire with creativity and love. We are then able to bestow gifts upon the earth and these we shower down onto the earth plane. These are divine catalysts of creative love, and they cause light and peace to be manifested within people's lives. For example, artists or musicians in various fields may suddenly receive longed for inspiration. Or a child may be born possessing the gift of a singing voice which will go on to bring succor to millions. Or rainbows imbued with ethereal light and color will appear as a reminder of God's love for humankind in various places on the earth. Such are the gifts that are regularly showered down from above as a result of our collective prayer in the life beyond death.

The connectedness on this side of being is often expressed in the form of a dance of the spheres. This quite took my breath away on the first occasion that I witnessed the phenomenon. The dance begins at the very center of all that is - within the Creator Himself. He initiates it entirely. This can begin at any moment - in response to the Creator's whim. One may perhaps think: how can the Creator dance or even want to dance in the face of all of the suffering that exists on the earth? But equally one could say: 'Why do birds bother to sing?' Or: 'Why does a butterfly bother to spread its wings and display its beauty?' All of these things happen simply because, in the face of all sorrow, joy still exists. There are essentially two sides to the coin of all life and creation. And so, the Creator begins His dance. This first starts as a murmur of sound and a veritable stirring within the waters of the vast sea which is God. Then this gradually grows and grows until one thinks that an explosion of sound and light must result. Imagine ripples slowly spreading across a pool and waves of sound and light beginning to travel outwards from the very center of all that is. When such an event begins to happen, we of AVESHIDA will be about our daily tasks. Then we will suddenly observe a stirring in the center of our deepest hearts. Thus one's foot may unconsciously begin to tap. Then another will begin to hum a tune, perhaps dimly remembered from long ago but not quite perceived. Then slowly, very slowly the sound and movement within one's being will begin to intensify, until one eventually finds that one cannot ignore it any longer. One will begin to move about a bit in time to the sound. Then all of a sudden the garments that one is wearing will begin gradually to change - for what we think we wear. My own clothes on such an occasion tend to be multicolored - all sorts of different hues. My robes reach to the ground and the material falls about my person in a comfortable and pleasing way. I also have golden dance slippers which are soft like a second skin. Then all of AVESHIDA congregate together of one accord and we begin our dance as a group. This is not like dancing on the earth but is a dance of souls, interweaving in and out of each other. Melding, first with one then with another. Knowing each other, yet not in a bodily way, but in the way of souls. Osmosis is the best way I can describe the phenomenon of meeting and knowing. Then, as we look upwards, we see that all of the heavens and all of the spheres are beginning to dance. The shining stars move and shimmer in time with the sound. The blue of the sky ripples with a million different shades of the one color - never static and always moving. And right across the heavens the sound gets louder, until it intensifies to a majestic pitch. Angels of gold appear out of nowhere, swooping, flying, laughing and exalting. Then the saints appear - not in bodily form, but their faces superimposed like a tapestry over the heavens. And so we, of

AVESHIDA, by this time are completely lost in sound, weaving in and out of one another in total synchrony of movement. And then, with a crescendo of sound, the King appears, His smile blessing and anointing us with joy. How long the dance goes on one cannot say, because, by this time we are beyond space and beyond all things. Eternal dance. Eternal joy. A showering of droplets of pure, pure love. If only I could convey it adequately; for words can only express the smallest part of it all, but maybe you are able to perceive the general idea?

4.

MY OWN ROAD TO CALVARY

Those of you who knew me, especially those who stayed with me in a supportive way during my final years on the earth, witnessed at first hand my own path of suffering during the last eleven years of my life. The nails driven into my hands were the disease Parkinson's - a devastating, creeping disorder that gradually took over my body and infiltrated my mind. It took away my independence and every facet of the previous enjoyment of my life on earth. I, a garrulous fellow, could no longer meet with and enjoy the company of friends in a social setting. My lot, very gradually, became that of a dependent invalid. To begin with I took on the 'why me?' stance and fought against all of this angrily. For even though as Christians we are programed, as it were, to endure our allotted suffering, when it comes upon us we are invariably unprepared and rebellious. The trusting abandonment of Our Lady is often not instantly the case in our own lives. But gradually, gradually, as one accepts and embraces the state of suffering and as one loves it as a path which is bringing us closer to God, deeper riches will come to light.

Throughout this period my soul center remained intact, but it became increasingly difficult for me to operate on a human level, due to the progressive depletion of my bodily functions. I also had to contend with the associated emotional problems which inevitably go hand in hand with the onset of severe disability. At the time of my diagnosis, I was pastor of a thriving London Church and spiritual director to numerous souls. I was involved in the healing ministry of the Anglican Church and I held positions of influence in several organizations of repute. But with the onset of disability, my situation began to change almost overnight and my condition caused me to struggle with the executing of my various responsibilities. My Church decided to 'let me go' in the nicest possible way, but as is usual in these situations, the outer niceties barely concealed the bitter pill of complete rejection that lay beneath. I found all of this understandably traumatic and I struggled with immense anger after being treated in what I felt was an unreasonable way. It felt that I had been marginalized because of my illness. Incidentally, this situation would not have been allowed to occur in such an insensitive way in a secular situation. Along with this state of affairs, some of those under my spiritual direction began to become embarrassed by my condition and to fall away. This all added up to a string of accumulated rejections that caused much pain. I felt that I wanted to cry out that I was still essentially the same person, but that I was imprisoned against my will within a body that was not capable of representing me any longer. It took a long time, as my illness progressed, for the flames of my anger and the sting of my hurt to simmer down to a controlled glow. Even at the moment of my passing much of this remained unhealed - I cannot deny this at all. However I must reiterate that I was also very fortunate to have many loyal friends who supported me faithfully throughout my ordeal.

During my former years of health and vitality; I would rush here and there preaching, ministering and healing. I was held in great acclaim by many and for a time I was something of a household name within the Anglican Church. I thought, at the beginning of my travail: 'God must surely mean me to write more books?' But then, even this outlet of creativity was taken away. My tremors became such that the holding of a pen became impossible. Then finally, my mind - the last vestige of dependability - refused to behave as it should. Memory became poor and eventually, nothing about my body was recognizable to me at all. I was in a foreign place. Indeed, I felt that I had 'died' even before my own death.

Where exactly was my soul while all of this was happening? Well, it was slightly above my body. Attached and beholden to the uselessness of my mortal frame.

And so I remained in this state of incapacity for some eleven years. My only real joy during this time were the occasions of visits of dear and trusted friends. Those who continued to look upon me as a valued and loved individual. Those who looked beyond the body of a decrepit invalid to the person within. For such is the case in every instance of the chronically sick and disabled. The person is held captive inside a mortal frame that no longer functions as it should.

But my life at that time was not all tragedy and I continued to pursue an active spiritual life. This area was in perfect working order and was not affected by my illness. In this respect, I remained completely whole and I thus continued with my work of healing and intercession.

For those of you reading this who do not know me at all, I will endeavor here to provide a few basic details about the beginnings of my life on the earth. If you wish to know more, I did write a number of other books that give the picture in a little more detail.[1]

During my years of ministry within the Anglican Communion, I have to say that I was always a worried priest. I did my work as it came to me, but I always felt 'awkward' in my own skin and I was never absolutely sure that I was getting it right. Was I doing the work intended for me? Had I got this right or that right? Was I failing miserably? It may surprise those of you who knew me to discover that I had no confidence in myself at all. I came across as irascible to many people, but I was in fact extremely shy and this shyness caused me to snap and grump at times. If only others had known what hidden agony I put myself through on a daily basis.

During my boyhood, alongside the episodes of appalling abuse inflicted upon me by my father, I experienced phenomena of a spiritual kind. I was visited by God. These meetings registered within my consciousness and gave me hope for the future. Hope that gave me the assurance, throughout the years of helplessness and powerlessness, that ultimately all would be well.

To begin with, I did not know God in a personal sense. To me He was simply an 'otherness' - an extreme power that seemed to exist apart from myself. God came to me especially during periods of relaxation when, as a boy alone in my room, I would listen to music. This had the effect of touching some sort of a 'trip switch' in my deepest consciousness which caused me to leave the material world - an environment that contained much fear and a burgeoning hatred within my young heart. I would thus enter an unseen world - a world of peace, of tranquility and perfect love. And there, within that love and safety, I found God's presence.

At this stage in my life I was, to all intents and purposes, a Jew. My mother and father were of the Jewish faith and during my childhood, we shared the traumatic knowledge that every one of our relatives in Lithuania was murdered by the Nazis. While we, in safety, languished in South Africa enjoying a wealthy lifestyle. This distant tragedy, incidentally, was the cause of my mother's labile emotional stability - an imbalance triggered by the knowledge that elsewhere the Holocaust was taking place. It instilled in her a haunting and perpetual fear that the cancer of this persecution and slaughter would eventually spread throughout the world and that it would reach our haven of security. My eventual forgiveness of my mother's blinkered attitude towards my own abuse came about because, at some level, I understood her need to maintain an outward facade of supposed perfection and normality. No excuse, I know, but this reason was there in her case. Anyway, to go on with my own story. I was a Jew and I was brought up as a Jew. But not an Orthodox Jew in any sense. Although I did, as was warranted by my father's standing, go through the process of bar mitzvah at the age of thirteen. We attended the synagogue, mainly because my parents wished to be seen to be doing the right thing within the community. But, in my own case, there was always a missing element within my Jewish faith. This was because of the immutable fact that, during my experiences of God, I invariably perceived the presence of a Person.

I was basically an inquisitive boy. I loved to read and to fill my head with facts and knowledge. It was during the course of my reading of the Scriptures, that I concluded that Jesus Christ and the Person whom I often encountered during prayer were one and the same. Thus the seeds of doubt regarding my inherited religion were steadily sown. I surmised that the reality of my spiritual encounters with the Personhood of Christ indicated that the Resurrection had indeed taken place. And so, my encounters with Christ and the accumulation of my related reading eventually led to a breaking away from the faith of my fathers and the development of my own personal Christian belief. I came to accept Jesus Christ as my personal Savior and I started to allow His healing to begin within me.

It was not until I reached adulthood that I fully acknowledged the immense anger pressed down inside me relating to the sexual abuse I had received as a child. When I discovered this I was frightened by its intensity. It seemed to be a 'super-anger' and an all pervading virulent rage. This was the anger of a man in relation to events that had occurred during childhood. I can honestly say that my anger was a murderous thing. When I perceived it, I could well imagine how one might come to commit the act of patricide. Not that I would ever have carried this out of course, but I could see the possibility of this crime if I had been a person with no religious faith or morals at all. More than anything I felt the need to rid myself as quickly as possible of the terrible burden of my own rage. I tried to see things from my father's point of view, but I was unable to imagine a valid reason for the committing of such terrible abuse upon one's own son. I would thus rail about it endlessly, running around in circles within my mind. Then, one day, during prayer, Christ Himself seemed to speak to me softly saying: 'What happened to you is essentially My affair. Leave all of the whys and wherefores to Me. All judgement ultimately belongs to God.' I then saw clearly that it is not our place to cast aspersions upon anyone else, however justified we might feel ourselves to be. And so, very slowly at first, I let God in. I handed over, as it were, all of my pain to God.

The Cross plays such a big part in the working through of this sort of trauma. For within the whole gamut of events surrounding the Cross, Christ Himself suffered every conceivable human assault at the hands of others. He was naked upon the Cross and exposed for all to see. He was shamed. There was no delicately and strategically placed loin cloth as our works of art would have us believe. The stark truth is that His own privacy was invaded just as in the case of a small child at the hands of a sexual abuser. On realizing this, I came to see that I could never look Christ in the eye and say: 'You don't know how it feels,' because He had already shared the agony upon the Cross along with myself and with all who have ever suffered this type of abuse. This realization was the first important step towards healing for me - the knowledge that Our Lord had 'been there too'. That He understood fully. It was then that the Lord seemed to reach out from the Cross and touch the heart of the wounded child that existed within me.

The tears I shed at that time seemed endless. I thought that they would surely never stop and for a while I feared for my own sanity. It seemed that the balance of my mind was disturbed by grief and pain and that I would never return to any sort of normality at all. It even felt that it would be preferable to return to the pre-discovery state - the stage before I had even acknowledged and 'owned' the abuse. At least at that time, the house of cards which constituted my mind had been upright and in order. Now these said cards lay scattered before me and I ultimately despaired of reconstructing any sort of order within my mind ever again. My very identity as a person seemed to be affected by the memories. For when one is abused, one's journey towards identity is halted. The abuser effectively causes an 'emergency stop' of one's emotional development. Thus, the fragile seedling of the delicate inner self becomes distorted and awry.

But recovery is possible and indeed was possible for me and the first step in my recovery lay in forgiveness.

5.

THE NATURE OF FORGIVENESS

In a situation where gross wrong has been committed, there is a tendency to think: 'surely forgiveness will be impossible in this particular case?' Indeed, in the face of any heinous crime, the concept of forgiveness may seem unthinkable. The crucifixion of Christ contained all of the elements of every wrong that it is possible to commit towards another human being. Yet Our Lord managed, at the height of His pain and suffering, to look upon his tormenting murderers and to bless them, saying: 'Father, forgive them; they do not know what they are doing.'[1] During my own earthly life, when I pondered about all of this in relation to my early experience of sexual abuse, I wondered: did my father, at the time of his wrongs towards me, really know what he was doing? Did he imagine at the time that he was burdening me with what would prove to be an unshakeable load - one that I would be forced to carry to the end of my life and beyond? Could he see that thereafter I would be condemned to a lifetime of inability to relate in an intimate way to anyone else in a normal human relationship of love? That he was destroying any chance of my successfully embarking on a path that could lead to the fathering of children of my own? No, I do not think that he knew this or indeed even considered it. I think that his only intention was the immediate satisfaction of his own distorted lustful desires. He probably imagined that, young as I was, I would later barely remember the acts at all. But abused children do not forget. Whether or not the crimes are remembered consciously, they will continue to affect the person at a very deep level. At the level of essential identity. Because sexual abuse introduces a type of 'echo' within the mind, which continues afterwards to resound in the depths of one's psyche. An echo that says: 'you do not matter at all, you are a thing and you are an object. Indeed, by these acts, I am saying that you are worthless as a human being.' This, then, is the stage that I myself had reached when I finally faced God fully with the burden of my own experience of abuse - a man in tears over the agony of the small wounded boy he once was.

Our Lord says: 'Let the children come to me; do not try to stop them; for the kingdom of Heaven belongs to such as these.'[2] And: 'if anyone causes the downfall of one of these little ones who believe in me, it would be better for him to have a millstone hung round his neck and be drowned in the depths of the sea.'[3] For no one 'gets away' with this sort of crime. All sins are eventually revisited upon the perpetrator and payment is demanded and required in full. But in the very act of forgiving the harm inflicted upon us, we are effectively releasing our abuser into the courts of God's own judgement. If we hold a crime committed against us within our own hearts and minds, we ultimately cause our own selves damage and we actively prevent God from dealing with the matter. Forgiveness therefore provides a fundamental release of responsibility to Almighty God. It constitutes a handing over of the prisoner that we have been holding within our own hearts into the dock of God's courthouse. If we are unable to do this, the very presence of the said prisoner will act like the seed of a cancer within our own souls. We need therefore to fully relinquish the cause of our pain to God in order to begin to allow His healing light to shine once again within our hearts. Forgiveness is an act that says: 'I hand all of this dear Lord into Your safekeeping. I want You to deal with it, for I myself cannot. I cannot hope to fully understand or to bring the matter to any sort of resolution at all. I cannot deal with this in my own human strength. It needs the touch of the Divine - Your touch.'

This type of release is intrinsically very powerful and it acts as a trigger mechanism. It basically gets our own selves out of the way and allows the influx of the Holy Spirit into the place of injury. And then finally, God's healing can begin. The poor shriveled seedling of one's inner self that has been hidden and obscured all of this time can at last stretch upwards towards the sunshine of God's love, unfurl its leaves and start to live again.

This is what happened to me. I myself got out of the way. For in these cases, while one is, of course, not essentially to blame, the ego is nevertheless heavily involved. An ego that says - 'I have a perfect right to judge my abuser and to bring this situation to justice. I have the right to seek out the perpetrator (if still on this earth) of the crime against me and to unleash my anger towards that person.' This should not be done. Handing over to God means exactly that. It means relinquishment. Total and absolute with no holds barred. Relinquishment in the full knowledge that God alone will fight one's corner. A God who has the ability to bring the situation to justice and to bring about recompense for the wrong actions committed. A God who will bring about all of the healing that is necessary within the situation.

One may wonder why sexual abuse has the propensity to damage the soul so deeply and lastingly. Why do such acts have the ability to cause such conscious and subconscious destruction? At its best, human sexual union is intended to be a profound gift of intimacy between two compatible individuals, allowing the fulfillment of the basic need to become one with the beloved. It is a surrender to the one whom one loves more than one's very soul. It is a type of 'dying'. Thus it is during the act of union that the soul is at its most vulnerable.

Sexual abuse normally comes about because of the presence of a deep wound within the abuser's own psyche. In all likelihood, a person who acts in this way has themselves been the recipient of such abuse in their own distant past. There are exceptions of course. There are criminal minds who act out evil for evil's sake. In some extreme cases, the occult is involved. But I wish here to concentrate on the effect that sexual abuse has upon the individuals concerned and why it has such a lasting effect upon those on whom it is inflicted.

The soul contains our spiritual 'DNA' and the blueprint of our own personal journey relating to our past, present and future. It is hidden and it is private, except to those with whom we wish to share it. It is directly linked to the Divine. In the anatomical sense, the soul is located centrally within the solar plexus area. When two people love each other very much, their relationship normally develops in stages. At first meeting there is a verbal sharing of mind meeting with mind. Profound excitement and recognition occurs when one encounters another human being with whom one shares a similar outlook and life experience. The discovery of a 'kindred spirit' as it were. And so, a friendship starts to develop which may eventually blossom into affection and love. There are, of course, different kinds of love. C. S. Lewis deals so excellently with this concept in his book 'The Four Loves,'[4] in which he describes affection, friendship, Eros and charity. Eros is experienced, in the first instance, as a type of 'sickness'. One yearns for the other person and the desire grows to spend increasing amounts of time in their company. Eventually, a bond may grow that is so deep that a sexual relationship will ensue. It is during sexual union that the souls of each person 'meet' in the deepest way possible. To illustrate this concept, imagine the analogy of a Venn diagram depicting two individual circles overlapping each another. The point of overlap signifies the union of the two different parts. Something of this sort occurs within the human soul during the act of sexual union. For a brief moment in time, two souls become one and the yearning within each heart is momentarily satisfied.

But what happens in the case of rape or sexual abuse? Well, in such instances the human soul is invaded by a perpetrator who is neither invited nor welcome. It is a 'burglary' of the worst possible sort. As such, the person's innermost soul is known (to use a Biblical term) by one who is of malign intent. By someone with whom one does not wish to share such a profound intimacy. It is an assault upon the victim's identity and upon all they essentially are.

During childhood, the soul is still in its developmental stage. A child has not yet had the chance to arrive at any measure of self-knowledge. The type of invasion afforded by sexual abuse is therefore particularly damaging and traumatic in the early years. To use an analogy, such an act could be compared to the intrusion of an unwelcome party into the darkroom of one's burgeoning soul. The place in which a work of something beautiful and unique is underway. All of a sudden this secret area is exposed and revealed by a malignly motivated and uninvited spotlight that is harsh and jarring. This results in the 'developing photograph' of the soul becoming distorted and overexposed. It causes severe damage. To use another illustrative analogy, one could picture a flowering bulb of the sort that needs darkness and warmth within its formative stages. Sexual abuse is akin to the violent flinging open of the protecting door of the darkened room and the callous invasion by the harshest of discordant lights.

Can this sort of damage be healed? Well, Scripture tells us: 'nothing is impossible to God.'[5] We are also told: 'Jesus Christ is the same yesterday, today and forever.'[6] God has the ability to reach back and to anoint such wounds in our distant past. He can flood the pain and the darkness with His healing and sanctifying light. God can make us whole.

How does God bring wholeness out of the devastating damage of sexual abuse? Well, the human memory and the power of the mind can be used to great advantage in such situations. Using the vehicle of the mind, God has the ability to travel back into the person's distant past and to change the soul's blueprint back to its intended perfection. God can reweave the discordant pattern of the travesty of human brokenness into something that is essentially more beautiful than the original. But first of all, forgiveness is necessary. Forgiveness is the key that has the ability to unlock the power of healing.

There are some psychological modes of thinking that would have one believe that, in the case of childhood sexual abuse, confrontation is necessary. That one should seek to face one's abuser and unload one's emotional burden of pain verbally. In other words, the opinion that there is no going forward until such a catharsis has been effected. But I myself do not believe that this is necessary. It should be enough to trust that God will take care of all that needs to be 'said' within the whole situation. That everything is safe within His healing hands. The main reason for this view is that it is only God who knows the heart and soul of the perpetrator of the said crime. He alone knows the full reason behind the abuse and we do not. He has the complete picture. All that we are required to do in such a situation is to let Christ in. And we, the abused, are the only ones who are able to do this. We hold the key to our own healing and until we get out of the way, God cannot do His work properly.

But how exactly do we begin to let God into our deepest pain? I would like to suggest an effective method that I used in my own case. This is a course of action that may be employed as soon as one has reached the stage of the acknowledgement of any area of pain within one's past. Incidentally, this need not necessarily be related to sexual abuse and could be anything which is the cause of injury or harm. In other words, the proverbial 'stone in one's shoe' in the emotional sense and the factor existing within one's past or present that is preventing one from going forward in a healthy and whole way.

The first step is to prayerfully bring the matter, whatever it might be, before God. The method that I used myself is known as 'imaginative prayer' - a tool that is often used within the context of an individually guided retreat. To those who are not familiar with the concept, this is a process that involves meditating prayerfully upon specific passages of Scripture, in order that their innate power may effect healing. If one has the assistance of a retreat director, such a person will be trained to choose an appropriate passage that is tailor made, as it were, for one's own situation. The Gospels and the Psalms are most often used. Alternatively, if the prayer takes place outside of a retreat situation, one should pray for the guidance of the Holy Spirit in the choosing of a Scripture passage for the purpose of a healing meditation.

Once an appropriate passage of Scripture has been decided upon, the next step is to thoroughly familiarize oneself with the passage, by reading it several times, before beginning to meditate upon it. Then, when a measure of stillness and prayerfulness has been arrived at, one should picture the scene as fully as possible, using the tool of one's imagination. In other words, one should create a clear image within one's mind of specific aspects within the scene, such as the weather, the place, the people and so on. Then one should try to be present within the imagined scene as fully as possible.

I would like now to give a direct example of such an experience from my own earthly healing journey. This took place when a close Christian friend, with whom I had shared my recollections of abuse, suggested that the method of imaginative prayer may be of help. The friend in question was Geoffrey, now one of my counterparts in the group soul AVESHIDA and with whom I had a close spiritual relationship during this particular period of my life on the earth. After praying together, Geoffrey felt inspired to suggest that I meditate upon the scene of Christ's crucifixion.

Thus I formed a picture in my imagination of the scene of the crucifixion. I imagined the weather as overcast and drizzly. I pictured the hordes of jeering masses around the Cross. I saw within my mind's eye those who were dear to Our Lord: His Blessed Mother, His family, His disciples and His friends. I imagined the Roman soldiers - how they were likely to have been dressed and their general demeanor. Lastly, I concentrated on the image of Our Lord on the Cross. As I focused on this image, I pictured the brutal nails driven into Our Lord's hands and feet, the crown of thorns upon His head, the blood running down His face and the emotional and spiritual pain etched on His features and reflected in His eyes. Then I began to imagine that I myself was present at the scene of the crucifixion - my boyhood self at the time of the sexual abuse - alone and in tears. I relived my feeling of utter isolation of that time, with no one reaching out to comfort or help me. In my imagination I - the boy I was then - stood weeping before the Cross. Then I chanced to look up at the Lord's dear face and into the eyes that gazed down upon me. As so often happens in this type of prayer, the scene suddenly began to take on a creative life of its own. I found that I was on the receiving end of a vivid experience during which Our Lord spoke to this inner child in a direct and personal way. Looking straight into the eyes of my sobbing, hurting boyhood self, He clearly said: 'Martin - you are My son.' From that moment I perceived a change beginning to take place within the depths of my wounded heart. In the middle of all of the negative emotions of despair, confusion and anxiety, a healing light began to spring into being. Then Our Lord spoke to His Mother, saying: 'You are this boy's Mother,' and He turned to the disciple John saying: 'You are this boy's brother.' In other words Our Lord reached directly back into my boyhood and gave me the gifts that I had most longed for and needed at the time of the abuse. As the Lord spoke the words: 'My son,' He effectively replaced my errant and abusive father with Himself. Then He gifted me with His own Mother - a Mother who would love and cherish me spiritually from that moment on. Lastly He gave me the spiritual companionship and friendship of a brother - His own dear friend John. In this way the painful events of my boyhood had all at once been deftly rewritten and essentially changed. The abusive acts themselves had not been erased, but the Lord Jesus Christ had Himself powerfully entered the memories and had profoundly and catalytically altered them.

When I eventually came out of the meditation, I found to my amazement that I was in a completely different 'place' in the emotional sense. The Lord had introduced a new functional family into my hurting memory banks, which had the effect of countering the negative dysfunction of those who had been responsible for me at that time. Thus it felt that I was now coming from a completely new place of existence. It is difficult to convey the incredible power of this mode of prayer which, in a miraculous way, enables the Holy Spirit to tangibly reach back into one's past and to effect healing - the healing of painful memories.

Geoffrey then suggested that an anointing with holy oil may be helpful in sealing and confirming the healing brought about by the meditation. Thus, in his capacity as a priest of the Anglican Church, Geoffrey administered the sacrament for me. This acted as an additional powerful tool and brought me comfort, healing and a deep sense of peace.

Later, in the privacy of my own heart, I had to reach a place of forgiveness of my father. This was a gradual process and one that was not fully complete until I eventually passed over to this side of being. During my earthly life, it seemed that every time I reached a point of forgiveness, a fresh surge of anger would rise up again and again. It felt that I was on a spiral of recurring anger, and I would repeatedly encounter the need to forgive and forgive and forgive again. And so, each time I perceived the presence of the anger within my psyche I would duly hand it over to God. Thus, bit by bit, God gradually took my anger into Himself and began to gently transform it with His healing touch. Ultimately, the only effective way to the healing of painful memories, whatever they may be, is regular daily prayer. The wounded area may also need to be explored in a counseling situation. But once this has been achieved, one should then try to refrain, if at all possible, from endlessly and perpetually going over the memories again and again in one's mind. Prayer is the only real way forward. Prayer will ensure the continued exposure of one's pain to God's light and love. Then, one day, either in this world or in the next, full healing and forgiveness will occur and one will achieve true liberation from the shackles of one's painful past.

Of course, in the area of sexual abuse, the memories never completely go away. They remain as a reminder of the pain of times past. But it is possible for their negative charge to be gradually nullified and the pain sanctified. As with the physical wounds of Our Lord, these emotional scars remain as a tangible reminder of the past from which one has journeyed in order to reach the present situation of grace within one's life. The very presence of these wounds forever after serves to instil humility within one's soul. One is reminded each day of the grace of Almighty God and all that one has to be thankful for.

6.

THE DEEPEST HEALING

By definition, death can perhaps best be described a baptism into the greater life. On passing through the portal of death, the soul immediately moves away from the body and progresses to a level corresponding to its individual development and receptivity to light and truth. Contrary to popular belief, the occurrence of physical death does not mean that all of one's problems and past errors immediately fall away. When a soul reaches the greater life, he or she will retain exactly the same psychological and spiritual state as was the case at the moment of death. There is a popular tendency on earth to 'deify' the recently departed and to attribute to them an instant state of sanctity. But after bodily death, one does not instantly move to a beatific state of wallowing among the clouds to the accompaniment of angelic harps. For what would be the point of existence at all, if, at the end of one's physical life, everything that had transpired during the earthly journey was immediately canceled out and nullified? No, the life beyond death is but a continuation of the soul's journey and as such one carries the accumulation of all of one's past life experiences, both positive and negative.

The human body basically consists of an intricate, interwoven structure of living machinery which contains a central life force. It acts as a protective tent which serves to sustain the soul during earthly existence. Despite extensive scientific research, many of its functions remain a total mystery and are completely beyond the scope of human understanding. For instance, no one has exact knowledge of the processes behind birth and death, or how the body heals and renews itself after injury. All explanation pertaining to this remains essentially hidden during one's earthly life. Each individual soul has an agenda of being and a blueprint of existence. Nothing ever happens by chance and even the appointed time of death is preordained and written in the Book of Life. This explains why some individuals cling tenaciously to earthly existence against all the odds while others, despite the best possible intervention of medical science, ultimately fail to survive.

Christian fundamentalists on the earth commonly assert the view that only believers in Christ may ultimately 'qualify' for entry into the Kingdom of Heaven. But progression in terms of the greater life has entirely to do with the state of one's innermost heart. Non-profession of belief in Christ will never in itself result in relegation to an eternity outside of the Heavenly Kingdom. How could this be the case when there are so many examples of non-Church-going individuals who live exemplary lives of love, kindness and charity? There are many outstanding individuals on the earth who, through no fault of their own, find themselves inwardly blocked in all areas that come under the general heading of 'religion'. All too often, trauma is experienced at the hands of the Church, which causes such internal barriers to be built. As a result, countless souls pass over to the greater life as questioners and seekers. But once a soul reaches this side of existence it becomes possible to encounter religious belief in its purest and most uncontaminated form. One is also afforded contact with higher souls whose radiance and love of God shine like a beacon for all to see and serve to lead the way forward. As is the case on the earth, the common denominator on this side of being is free will, in terms of individual belief, and the personal response of each soul to goodness and truth is awaited. Each soul is given the choice of opting to remain on the lower levels of eternity and may ultimately decide to deny soul progression altogether if they so wish. In the general sense, everyone is aware of instances on the earth of those professing belief in Christ, while at the same time displaying behavior which is less than Christian. In its most extreme form, this may sometimes extend to committing acts of rank cruelty and lack of love. But Christian and non-Christian souls are ultimately accountable for their every thought and action, both good and bad, and there exists a law of cause and effect. This means that whatever one does during one's life on the earth, positive or negative, is incorporated into the cosmic consciousness and will have consequences.

The question of rebirth has always been a controversial issue within the Christian Church, while it remains an accepted belief in other major religions. The Buddhists and the Hindus are only too aware of the truth of the concept, but for many Christians this is a mode of thinking that remains somewhat touchy and nebulous. I can positively confirm that souls do return to the earth and that rebirth does take place. There will also come a time, as in the cases of the members of our group, when the rebirth cycle ceases altogether and the earthly journey is complete.

The life of the individual soul comprises an endless tapestry of interwoven threads, with each tiny thread representing every nuance and sigh of human existence. At its conception, the newly created soul displays a pattern that is pleasing to behold. But once a wrong or negative deed is committed this results in the development of an ugly knot. The person may try to rectify matters themselves, but in doing so they risk breaking the thread sequence completely. The only possible way that the overall pattern can be properly corrected is for the affected line of work to be completely undone and for a new thread to be attached. Thus the section is begun again so that the whole pattern can be re-perfected and re-formed.

At the beginning of their time on the earth, souls are effectively empty books on which nothing has yet been written. But imagine the scenario of an individual having taken a wrong turn. Perhaps, on reaching adolescence, the person may become a bully and may terrorize their fellows with emotional, psychological and physical cruelty and abuse. When such an individual reaches adulthood, they may then attempt to reform by kicking over all traces of their wrong doing. They may resolve to turn over a new leaf and try to proceed with their life as if nothing negative had occurred. But the truth will out as they say and all errant behavior and wrongdoing will already have been indelibly recorded in the Book of Life. In other words, the person's copybook will have been irrevocably blotted and the aforementioned tapestry of the soul will then contain a nasty lump of discordant threads that spoils the overall pattern completely. Ostensibly, such a person may perceive themselves as having moved on to an entirely new situation. They may perhaps breathe a sigh of relief and inwardly consider: 'I got away with all of that - it is now hidden in the past and forgotten about. I need never think of it again.' But by virtue of the law of cause and effect, this can never be the case. All is noted and recorded. Every breath that one takes is of infinite importance. The record of wrong behavior will have irretrievably altered the divine blueprint of such a person's existence, and at some stage they will be required to experience every ounce of trauma inflicted on those they have previously wronged. Fundamentalist Christians may protest at this point and may assert that the doctrine of redemption and forgiveness dispenses with the need for all of this. It is indeed true that one will ultimately be forgiven, once one reaches an attitude of true repentance for any wrongdoing that one has committed. But the fact remains that one will also be required to experience every iota of harm that one has inflicted upon one's fellows. There is simply no getting away from it at all - this is just the way that things happen and the way it is.

If one has suffered woundedness during earthly life this does not necessarily have to lead to the inflicting of harm on others. My own early life is a case in point. With my background of abuse during childhood, things could have turned out quite differently for me. I could conceivably have used this as an excuse, as it were, for errant behavior and depravity of my own. In other words I could have revisited the sins committed towards me on other hapless individuals, thus allowing my own woundedness to stretch on ad infinitum. But I did not let this happen. The reason for this was that during my early life I perceived the existence and reality of God and I responded to this perception by going on to live my life in the light of this knowledge.

By definition, each individual soul is entirely unique and each contains the divine spark - that which connects it to God. During the earthly lifetime, the soul is connected to the body by a type of thread that is commonly known on this side of being as the etheric cord. After death, this structure, which connects soul to body in the area of the solar plexus, immediately begins to dissolve. On passing through the curtain of death, the spiritual body will prove to be identical in outward appearance to the physical body just vacated, which comes as a surprise to many. Once the detachment of the etheric cord is complete, one then experiences a feeling of weightlessness. The same faculties are retained and one is able to see, hear and perceive in exactly the same way as before. (It is therefore extremely important to be careful what one says around the body of a recently deceased person). If the passing has taken place in a hospital setting and death is untimely and unexpected, one may then observe medical personnel in a great frenzy of activity around one's mortal frame. The cocoon of one's body will be visible lying motionless in the place where death has occurred. One will also observe the presence of a light, which denotes the doorway between this world and the next and there will be a strong inner intimation of the necessity to step through this doorway. Once this has been achieved, there will ensue a period of rapid traveling towards the next sphere of being. This is a completely painless process and is really rather liberating and pleasant. Having passed through the tunnel connecting the earth plane to the greater life, one normally arrives in a nebulous misty plane where the terrain appears dulled and muted. This effect is quite deliberate and is provided in order to soften and lessen the shock of transition. There one will meet with a supportive and nurturing presence - a being of light, a loved family member or friend, an angelic presence or someone who seems essentially familiar, but whose identity remains perplexingly elusive to begin with. This allocated 'receiver' is the one who will provide assistance through the initial stages of the ongoing journey. Before the moment of death itself, there may sometimes be a presentiment of this initial meeting. A terminally ill patient will often report the manifestation of a positive presence as the time of death draws near - perhaps an angel or a deceased loved one. This has the effect of preparing the consciousness for the forthcoming journey and serves to bring great comfort to the dying person. Incidentally, following one's passing, there will be ample time and space for reunion with loved ones. But then one will progress to a place of rehabilitation so that one may adjust to the transition. Thus, each soul first gravitates to a place of 'assessment'. This may sound rather grim and may perhaps conjure up a negative picture of some sort of a 'correctional facility', but this is not the case. These are places of light, healing and peace and are populated by souls of a higher plane. Here, advanced souls help 'new arrivals' to review their lives on earth in order to discern where help and healing is specifically needed. Issues are looked at honestly, intelligently and most importantly, with compassion. For all of us, on this side of being, are moving steadily towards the light and love of God, but we cannot make any real progress until every painful factor within our lives has been resolved, reconciled and made whole. Once a soul passes over to the greater life, the journey towards healing and wholeness continues seamlessly onwards. If inner woundedness is a factor, there exist mansions of healing on every level of existence, which provide ministry for the various hurts and traumas sustained during earthly life. As mentioned previously, I myself was in need of such respite and reintegration following the completion of my work on the earth. Some souls simply need complete rest initially as the whole process of dying and death is extremely exhausting to the soul. Sleep is a true healer on this side of being also. Other souls are anxious to look around, to get their bearings and generally orientate themselves. Their immediate wish is to discover what the greater life means and they crave answers to all of their questions. Yet others are so traumatized by the events leading up to their passing, that healing is what they require most in the first instance. In general it takes time to properly acclimatize oneself to the very fact that one has died. It is an overwhelming shock to begin with and there may be a period of disorientation and perhaps rebellion within one's soul, especially if death was sudden and unexpected. There will also remain an inevitable attachment to the earth - for the individuals one has left behind and for one's former way of life. The newly deceased have to cope with the trauma of parting with loved ones and bereavement and mourning do not only take place on the earth plane. However, on reaching this side of being, one will have the opportunity to spend time with loved ones who are already established here and this will serve to soften the blow of parting with those who have been dear on the earth. Great comfort is received by the new certainty of knowledge that life after death is a potent reality and that ultimately one can look forward to being reunited with all of those with whom one has shared a bond of love on the earth.

So, to begin with, the soul will normally reside for a period in the reception sphere on the level that is specific to their individual stage of soul development. Here the soul is assisted to become fully acclimatized to its new state of being. If passing has been the result of a serious physical illness, healing for this will need to take place. The malignancy of illness, both physical and psychological, has the effect of transmuting the mortal frame and affects the essential being which is the soul. The soul will thus have received something of a 'battering' both physically and psychologically. The mansions of rest and healing on the reception planes of each sphere appear as tranquil buildings to which the advanced souls of light constantly come and go in ministry. Within the mansion, one is given a spacious room which proves both congenial and comfortable. There will be personal touches relating to one's former existence and the decor will have been prepared sensitively and thoughtfully. Nothing, on this side of being, is too much trouble and everything is motivated by love. The view through one's window will be healing in itself and upbuilding to the soul. The time spent in the mansion will be geared entirely towards rest and recuperation from the traumas of one's lifetime on the earth and the shock of transition to the greater life. There will often be tangles pertaining to relationships which may have accumulated during the course of one's lifetime on the earth and which create unresolved issues on various levels. On this side of life, one is encouraged to reach a peaceful conclusion with all who were adversaries while on the earth. Only when such matters have been addressed and ironed out will one be able to move forward in a harmonious way. This can be all rather traumatic, but help and support is given in the form of the intermediating ministry of the higher souls of light, of which Maccabee is an example within our group. Shortly after my own passing, I was required to undertake a series of encounters with significant others with whom I had been connected while on the earth. Those, in other words, with whom I had 'issues' and with whom I needed to make peace before I was able freely to move on. I won't go into detail about all of this. It may make tedious reading in any case, for it was entirely personal.

And so, the soul moves on, beginning to make progress and gradually starting to familiarize itself with the unfolding picture of all that the life of eternity holds in store. The new adventure has finally begun. One's cup truly starts to brim over.

7.

FURTHER IN

When a wounded soul arrives on this side of being, he or she is allocated a mentor who is experienced in the transitional process, so that everything can be gently addressed and brought to healing. This process may be long or short depending on individual receptivity and progress. But in the greater life, 'time' does not matter at all and nobody is rushed in any sense - one may take as long as one likes. It will also be possible to receive visits from loved ones already on this side of being and as one progresses and becomes inwardly stronger, one will be able to pay them visits also.

What 'form' is one in at this stage and how does one appear in the outward sense? Well, on reaching eternity one inhabits a spiritual body that is not formed of solid matter, as is the case on the earth, but of a substance entirely spiritual. Perhaps the best way to explain this is to say that there exists an osmotic field in the next plane of being. When a person dies and vacates their mortal frame, that which is solid matter is left behind in the earth's atmosphere and that which is spiritual moves forwards to occupy the new empty space around the soul. Spiritual particles osmotically fill up the exact amount of space that has been vacated by the mortal body, so that initially one resembles exactly the frame one has left behind. As mentioned earlier, as one progresses, 'age' here is a matter of personal choice. I, for instance, am much 'younger' now - in outward appearance at least. I have more hair for example - an esthetically pleasing point! We choose the 'age' of our spiritual embodiment - although of course age means nothing here as we have perpetual longevity. Incidentally, my name continues to be Martin, but I do have other names too. But to refer to me as 'Martin' is still appropriate and I still answer to this. Basically, one is allowed to choose the incarnation one favored most while on the earth. I chose to be around 'thirty' when I passed over because it seemed to me to be an optimum age. Our Lord was thirty-three for example at the end of His earthly existence. But in terms of inner progression one remains in exactly the same place when one passes over.

In terms of environment on this side of being, how are the spheres structured? The earth plane is effectively a place of solid, tangible matter where understanding and perception is limited. The spheres, however, are much deeper than one could ever imagine. They go on forever, have countless levels and are essentially created by the souls themselves. It is really very complex as a concept, but this is how I would put it simply. The spheres comprise schools of souls at differing stages of progress. Then beneath the earth plane are what are known as the lower regions. These are the planes of darkness and again there are many layers therein which progress down to the final abyss. I will not dwell on this subject at this stage, but I will explain more about it later on. Suffice it to say that this is an unhappy area of trapped souls - trapped, I mean, by their own will and volition. This is where we as a group do most of our spiritual work. It needs also to be mentioned at this point that the prayers of those on the earth for such struggling souls are vital and powerful. Much of my own spiritual work on the earth was concerned with intercession for souls in these lower regions. My 'boatman' work for instance consisted of prayers of healing to effect release to those who were trapped. Every soul in the lower regions has essentially created their own form of hell.

Shortly after I arrived I began to meet up with many I had known before. I was actually amazed at my reception as I really hadn't perceived myself as being that popular. As mentioned before, I had always considered myself to be rather an irascible individual and somewhat 'prickly'. But despite this, there were many on hand to welcome me. To begin with I did not notice much at all due to my sensitive state. This made things very painful I must admit. There were no harps and gentle lullabies after my passing and there was a veritable baptism of the fires of revelation and exposure and of everyone seeing me exactly as I am. Despite my belief and despite my faith, at the moment before I passed over, I have to admit that I was afraid. I am thoroughly ashamed of this fact now of course. But I think that everyone without exception does experience a modicum of fear at that moment, however strong their faith and belief in God. As previously stated, the process of leaving my physical body was akin to a type of slipping away and a passing from one room to the next. In the physical sense, the last days of my illness on the earth had been extremely difficult on many levels. My incapacity had become an interminable trial of drooling, sniffling and constantly wetting myself. For someone as immaculate as I liked to be this proved to be very traumatic indeed. But thankfully, during this time, I was able to enjoy the visits of dear friends who saw beyond the incapacity to the truth of the person beneath. Overall, my last illness constituted a sort of desert period, during which I was denied the pleasure of the normal course of everyday living and the distractions that exist therein. I had to face my own demons so to speak and a lot of prayer went on during my time of enforced solitude or relative solitude. I slept a great deal during my latter years - not only due to the Parkinson's, but because of the accelerated spiritual healing that I was going through. It all proved quite exhausting. I admit that during my latter years on the earth I often wished, in the physical sense, to give up entirely and to abandon myself to the illness. Sometimes it felt that it would be infinitely preferable to give in and to take to my bed like a babbling invalid. But that would have been the easy way out and a succumbing. Somehow, and I really don't know how, I managed to remain in my place of prayer with my eyes fixed on the light, witnessing the way home to all who visited me. In the general sense, when traversing dark valleys of trial and tribulation, one does well to remember Christ in His darkest hour. The time when He shouted: 'My God, my God, why have you forsaken Me?'[1] One should try to echo His cry into one's own darkness and it may then become possible to begin to personally identify with Christ in His prayer of desolation. This will serve gradually to batter the darkness and will afford glimmers of healing light.

In the cycle of rebirth, one may wonder how a soul is later recognizable to those he or she has previously known and loved in other lifetimes? Once a soul has returned to the earth and has adopted a new outer form as it were and has begun to exist within an entirely new situation, will he or she then cease to be the person that they were previously? Well, there is no need to be anxious on that score. The essential soul center remains the same and will continue to shine outwards in its own unique way, so that the individual will remain instantly recognizable and familiar to all who previously held them dear. At a future time, reunions will take place with all of those to whom the soul was connected by love in each previous existence. The fact of the matter is that in the case of each soul, there will always be one identity, no matter how many incarnations have previously taken place. Consider the account in the Gospels - the time at which, following Our Lord's resurrection, He encountered Mary Magdalene in the garden. We are told that Mary: 'saw Jesus standing there, but she did not recognize him.'[2] Then still later, two of the disciples also encountered the Lord on the road to Emmaus. We are told: 'something prevented them from recognizing him.'[3] The reason for the lack of recognition in both of these instances was that the outward appearance of Jesus had essentially changed. He remained inwardly the same Lord, but His outward appearance was so altered that it was only when He performed a familiar action: 'he took bread and said the blessing; he broke the bread, and offered it to them,'[4] that they recognized it to be Jesus at all. This will be the case with all with whom we are reunited beyond death. As previously mentioned, we will be allowed to choose our outward form from our previous bodily incarnations. But it is very common for souls to choose to inhabit the appearance of their most recent earthly tent. The reason being that this will have pleasant associations and will relate to the time of the soul's optimum stage of spiritual development upon the earth.

The nature of the rebirth of an individual soul is decided on in collaboration with the higher echelons of light. When a soul passes over to this side of being, a review will take place pertaining to the life just completed and this will be followed by the aforementioned healing process to repair any pain and distress therein. Following this, consideration will be given as to what is needed to assist the soul on its journey towards the farther reaches of light. For there is ultimately an 'end product' and an optimum level towards which each soul is progressing. Incidentally, in the collective sense, we as a group have now reached this optimum stage. We are now in the pre-illumination stage - that which comes directly prior to absorption into the light of God. This may perhaps sound rather alarming, but no fear is necessary at all. The word 'absorption' may seem to infer that one will cease to be oneself altogether, but this is not the case. All that will happen is that in becoming actualized one will become a purer version of oneself. In other words, one will reach the full potential of one's being. Within our group, Maccabee is a prime example of such a light-filled state. As previously mentioned he is a soul whose home is within the farther reaches of the light of God and he returns to help us in our work. Effectively, he acts as a grounding element for our group and is rooted in the farther light. Thus we borrow him, so to speak, during our rescue work and he also joins us during our collective sessions of prayer. He is somewhat elusive and mysterious and it is never possible to pin him down in any sense. We simply gratefully accept his presence among us when he is there and we do not question the lack of his presence when he is not.

So, in each instance, the rebirth process is thoroughly discussed with each soul. This provides complete understanding of the reasoning and necessity behind entry into a particular life situation. Essentially, each individual soul craves progression overall. Once a soul is reborn, all memory of this side of being is temporarily erased. Except in the case of very advanced souls, who are permitted to reach realization of such information for the purpose of aiding the work that they need to complete on the earth. But in general, souls are unaware from whence they came. This spiritual blindfolding is very necessary, because the purpose of life on the earth is the purification of the soul. This is a process that must happen spontaneously and each soul must find its own way back to the light of God without the help of prior knowledge or intent. It must happen entirely of the soul's own accord and volition and must transpire purely through the motive of love - the love of God, the love of one's fellows and the love of oneself. In relation to good and evil and darkness and light, each soul must choose, independently of any outward influence or design, the direction in which they wish to travel in each life situation they are presented with.

Prior to re-entry into the earth plane, the soul is thoroughly prepared for the life that they are about to commence. The purpose and reasoning behind the rebirth is discussed and they will also be shown their sealed orders and their raison d'être, as it were. In some cases the ensuing lifetime will be short and in others the soul will return for a normal span. In some cases the life will be extraordinary in human terms and in others it may appear to be comparatively ordinary. But in reality there is essentially no 'ordinariness' at all within the light of God's infinite love. Each soul is cherished by God, made by Him and ultimately belongs to Him. And on behalf of each individual soul, Christ has died and has risen again.

During my time as spiritual director on the earth, I sometimes had occasion to guide souls through experiences of recollection of previous existences. In such instances, my initial role was one of reassurance. But once this had been given and the person concerned had been given permission, as it were, to relax into the unfolding experience, there often evolved a fascinating sequence of recollections which led to healing of any pain contained therein. Once the recollections had run their course, the individual would often report back that all previously unexplained inner turmoil had now stilled and that they perceived a sense of wholeness within that had never previously been known to them. Accompanying such journeys always proved to be a very great gift and had the effect of strengthening my own faith and knowledge. Indeed, in general I always found it a tremendous privilege to be allowed hallowed access into the spiritual life of another.

My own belief on the earth was always centered on a personal faith in Jesus Christ as Lord and Savior. But I also believed that there is ultimately no right or wrong path in the spiritual sense and that each mode of religious belief has something of importance to teach and to offer. In the Gospels, Our Lord clearly referred to the existence of other authentic ways apart from the Christian way, which provide a valid path towards light and truth of being. Once one reaches the higher planes of existence one sees very clearly that this is so. On this side of being, for example, one of the higher beings of light is Gautama Buddha. He has many followers on the earth and many who emulate his sacred path. The fundamentalist Christians on the earth generally assert that it is only by believing in Christ that one can be assured of eternal life, but they are really being far too simplistic. The Buddhist believers will, when they pass to this side of being, eventually encounter Gautama Buddha and they will also encounter the Christ. All will ultimately be one with no division. We should always strive to respect one another's spiritual paths because what is right for one may not be right for another. Each one of us, whatever the outward 'packaging' of our chosen religion, is essentially journeying into light and truth of being. There are also those on the earth with no professed belief at all - the atheists and the agnostics. Many such people in fact worship their own selves on a self-fashioned throne of kingship. They argue with great fervor and conviction about the lack of a God in the universe, but there is a lot that they cannot ultimately explain. For instance the origins of humankind, the healing powers of the human body and Christ's Resurrection. The latter is a historical fact which they manage to skirt over pretty neatly. Christ's case cannot be fought on intellectual soil and, while on the earth, His truth can only be found in the depths of the human heart.

In attempting to describe the rebirth process, it is perhaps useful to imagine the structure of a wheel and to see the soul as the center of that wheel. Thus each instance of rebirth takes place on the circumference of the wheel, but the central soul that forms the axis remains firmly in place in each instance of rebirth. The soul is therefore the nucleus. The reason why Our Lord was unrecognized by His disciples following His resurrection was because He had by that time reverted to the nucleus of His essential self. It is true to say that the more advanced the soul, the more perfect and greater are the tasks carried out by that soul. Our Lord, of course, was the ultimate example in His sacrifice on behalf of humankind. But others too have come and have not been recognized. Such souls have been planted in all manner of tragic situations and all manner of virtual crucifixions have taken place. Take, for example, the major trials endured by the human race during the Holocaust. There were many soul extensions in this situation who remained connected to the nuclei of their mother souls among the communion of saints on this side of being. These souls acted as catalysts, serving to siphon pain away from this tragic situation. In all such instances, these higher echelons of light remain docked to their soul nuclei on this side of being. During the tragedy of the Holocaust, many soul extensions were born on the earth specifically to bring comfort, healing and strength to those who suffered within the Nazi death camps. At the time of this atrocity I was a teenager in South Africa and I formed a spiritual link with one such soul extension. My developing psychic sensitivity meant that I was all too aware of the situation of unrest spreading throughout Europe. During my times of prayer I gradually became aware of my spiritual link with this particular soul existing in the middle of the horrific situation. Interiorly, I began to share that person's suffering. This was to prove to be one of the first instances of my 'boatman' work, which later became an intrinsic factor of my Christian ministry of prayer and intercession. On the day of the said soul's earthly death, I was able to journey spiritually to the other side of being and found the soul in a grossly injured state. I was then able to aid the soul's progression towards the light. In some cases, following a period of healing, a soul extension may then subsequently choose to be reborn upon the earth, while carrying the memory of the pain they previously suffered. In acknowledging, experiencing and working through such inner pain on the earth plane, such souls are then able to transmit waves of peace and healing into the collective consciousness, which will eventually serve to bring collective healing to many.

Earthly existence can perhaps be simplistically compared to a darkened room which, at the moment of death, becomes infused with brilliant light. At this moment, that which was previously invisible then immediately becomes visible. This is the basic difference between earthly life and the life of eternity - one is able to see clearly once the light has been switched on. Death ultimately provides the light that enables one to fully see.

8.

THE MIRACLE OF THE ATONEMENT

Modern society tends towards an unconditional adulation of the rich and the famous, perceiving them to be infallible oracles on every conceivable topic. But closer examination of the lives of such individuals, although they appear on the surface to contain all that is essentially desirable, often reveals a profound inner poverty. If this were not the case, why do so many seek destructive solace from sources such as excessive sexual gratification and substance abuse? The modern expectation is for every desire to be quenched on demand, a mindset that so often leads to crime against the human person. On a daily basis one is bombarded by media reports of violence, coercion, theft, humiliation and degradation - wrongs that are all too frequently initiated by differences in color, sexual orientation, age and gender. But such ills can often be sourced to spiritual deficiency and a deep emotional woundedness.

Since the very beginning of time, world rulers have striven to maintain societal precedence by blatant displays of accumulated wealth. But history categorically reveals that no earthbound acquisition ultimately proves equal to the boundless and enduring treasure of love. Thus the human heart is doomed to remain homeless and unsatisfied unless it is rooted in a relationship of love with its Creator. Union with the Divine alone serves to actualize the presence of uncreated love in the soul and bring about positive fruit in the periphery of one's human relationships. But why, one may conceivably ask, should Almighty God desire to seek a relationship of love with notoriously fickle and unreliable human beings? The answer is that He has a longing to endow the human race with that most priceless of all gifts - unconditional perfect love. This will have the effect of transforming the divine spark in the human heart into a roaring unquenchable bonfire. If such a state were ever to be achieved on a global level, the result would be the illumination of the whole world.

Throughout human history, the inhabitants of the world have striven tirelessly to harness every available source of power, but still the most enduring of all the earth's resources remains largely untapped - the self-perpetuating energy of love. Every human journey can be said to be basically defined by a quest for love - whether consciously acknowledged or not. It is true to say that most individuals, when challenged to describe the exact nature of their deepest need, are at a loss to provide a comprehensive answer. However, even the most blatantly materially orientated individual harbors a secret longing for this most elusive of all gifts, which alone has the potential to give meaning and truth to all other aspects of human existence.

In the midst of the varying twists and turns of the earthly journey, love often reveals itself most clearly at times of gross tragedy or misfortune, either in one's own life or in the lives of those one holds most dear. Here, in the perilous quicksands of human hopelessness, the pacifiers and sops of the tangible world suddenly fade into insignificance and lose all of their attraction and drawing power. Somewhere, in the depths of the afflicted heart, a cry for help comes forth, often without any expectation of an answer. When a tangible lifeline miraculously appears, the recipient may at first doubt its validity. But thankfully the Author of Life is never fazed by such initial cursory dismissal. He is so helplessly besotted with each human soul that none of this is important to Him.

All that is of interest is the prospect of offering a warm welcome home into the safety of His Father's heart. The suffering soul may perhaps question God's motive, asking something along the lines of: 'What is in it for Him?' But the answer to this is very simple - He wishes to wrap His love around the soul like a protecting cloak and hold it in an embrace of tenderness that will never let go.

A life changing event of this sort took place in the lifetime of St Paul - a highly unpleasant individual until the time of his vision on the Damascus road.[1] But his position and influence proved to be of little use when he was rendered blind and helpless in the space of one moment in time. His only option at this juncture was to humbly follow the instructions given by the very Lord he had been persecuting. Indeed, so complete was his incapacity that he had no other choice. He had to trust and he knew within his heart - a place he had never examined closely before - that it was right to do so. As a result, his life was transformed. It is the same potentially in the case of every individual on the earth. One is able to receive, at times of humiliation, brokenness and despair, the means to change direction. Not everyone receives a dramatic outward vision as in the case of St Paul. With some the experience is more subtle and hidden, but meaningful just the same in that it marks the advent of a new chapter in the person's life. This, then, is the purpose of each and every human pilgrimage on earth - to provide the opportunity of encountering the One to whom one owes one's very existence. And once we abandon ourselves to the embrace of the 'everlasting arms',[2] we will at last begin to be powerfully transformed into the people we were always meant to be.

During one earth-shattering moment over two thousand years ago, the most perfect example of love in action occurred in the very midst of the human race. It consisted of an act of self-emptying abandonment on behalf of others and held in wounded hands the essential nature of love with all of its intricacies and possibilities. Here the finite heart was terminally shattered and the Word of God proceeded to etch an indelible invitation at the very center of the collective human consciousness. The momentum behind all of this was the kernel of pure undiluted love within the heart of the uncreated God.

Love was the very nature of the Cross, but there are few in today's world who are cognizant of its real significance. The familiarity of the story causes many to gloss over the facts without any depth of understanding at all and there is a resulting failure to comprehend true meaning. However, most people have at least a basic knowledge of the events that unfolded all that time ago. Most, for example, are familiar with the identity of the faithful mother who stood watching in the shadow of the towering infrastructure of human brutality, as the lifeblood of her beloved child flowed away. As every parent can attest, there is nothing more agonizingly painful than to helplessly witness the suffering of one's own daughter or son. This mother's pain was further intensified by the fact that she was out of reach of all touch and whispered encouragement, her only possible mode of communication being that of heart speaking to heart. Every experience of suffering on the earth eventually became distilled within Christ's penultimate cry upon the Cross: 'My God, my God, why have you forsaken me?'[3] But was this a very human expression of unadulterated despair, or did it possess a deeper meaning? In fact, this juncture of human history constituted the crucial turning point of the human race. At this moment, for the merest nanosecond, God Himself died. One may assert that surely Almighty God could never die and that this would be a complete impossibility. But to discover the truth of what actually occurred, it is necessary to look at the concept of the Trinity - a doctrine that has persisted in baffling theologians and lay Christians alike for centuries. For within the divine mystery of the Trinity lies the essential truth of the crucifixion. It is here that the impossible begins to become possible.

By virtue of the Trinitarian mystery, Almighty God was able to die, remain alive and to resurrect all at the same moment in time. God the Son cried out in anguish on the Cross, while bearing the entire load of human decay, weakness, sin and suffering. God, the Father turned His face away, unable, in His state of divinity, to look upon that which had become no longer divine, by virtue of human sin. (The latter not in any judgemental sense, but due to the fact that His divinity precluded Him from processing any imperfection at all). And God the Holy Spirit began to flow unimpeded through the heart and veins of the crucified one. Thus the human flesh of Christ began to become transformed into transubstantiated matter - which would ultimately permit Him to rise, bloom into new life and to pour His blessings upon humankind.

During Old Testament times, Abraham, the father of the Jewish race showed his own willingness to sacrifice his son if God so willed it.[4] In this story, Abraham's dedication to God became evident. The relevance of the illustration pertains to the love behind his response. But, in the case of Christ's death on the Cross, there was no staying hand and no one to say: 'Stop - this is not necessary after all.' Almighty God was required to relinquish His beloved Son and was forced to watch His agony, while at the same time experiencing all of the pain of a devastated parent. The motivation behind this sacrifice was purely and simply - love. Christ's willing death created a doorway that would ultimately offer humankind a place in eternity. The miracle of the Atonement had begun.

The immensity of this event gave rise to a whole gamut of physical manifestations. Tombs broke open. Shining stars were blinded. The light of the sun was quenched. The life force of the universe was completely switched off. As a result, all light ceased, all warmth disappeared and all love failed. The inhabitants of the earth were sustained during this period by the energy that already existed in the center of their beings. There occurred an eclipse on the earth of all that was essentially divine. For a time nothing breathed and the engines of primary existence palled and threatened to collapse. The moment of extreme definition arrived when: 'the curtain of the temple was torn in two.'[5] At this instant; humankind had the ability to be free. The travesty of the Cross had become the gateway to the Father's heart.

Forever after, the mystery and the power of the Cross was able to be perpetuated on the earth through the enduring legacy of the Holy Mass. Substances of the earth thereafter had the ability to be transformed and made heavenly. Christ's victory allowed divine life to be married to the finite and to be engraved upon the spiritual blueprint of the earth.

9.

THE ETERNAL LEGACY

The miracle of the Holy Mass allows the admission of a chink of pure divine light into the darkness and desperation of this sullied world. It facilitates a process in which the sacred presence of the resurrected Christ is able to directly transform the earthly elements of bread and wine. The very act of consuming in faith the spiritual manifestation of Christ allows His entry into the believing heart.

By definition, the process of transubstantiation[1] is all to do with doorways and the creation of doorways. Infinity is enabled to enter the finite and is able to bind with that which is of the earth. The matter of the elements is transformed from dull substances of the earth - from that which will die - into Something More.

Before His crucifixion, Christ, in the physical sense, was formed of that which is of the earth. He trod our ground and He shared our life. He took part in every possible human trial and ultimately triumphed over all. But the sheer forsaken darkness of the moment of His death led to a blanking out of sun and moon and an eclipse of all that was divine on the earth. It caused everything to stop and for a time nothing breathed. There occurred a significant pause and the very engines of life and primary existence threatened to collapse. Because His was a willing death that constituted a total surrender, a spiritual doorway was created. This opened up the possibility of the transformation of earthly matter into that which is divine. Christ's death facilitated an onrush and admission of divine life into the finite blueprint. He created the possibility, by consecration and priestly authority, of transforming the finite matter of the elements through the Eucharistic blessing into that which is infinite.

Following consecration, to all intents and purposes, the matter of the bread and wine looks the same, but it is essentially not. The very act of consuming in faith Christ's eternity, Christ's divinity and Christ's possibility allows His entry into the believing heart and enables Him to anoint the soul. It matters not at what state or spiritual stage one exists, although one hopes that confession of fault has preceded the grace of consumption. The gift of the Holy Mass allows divinity to enter the mortal frame and allows it to bind with that which is of the earth. The sacramental leaven contained in the dull heaviness of the dough creates the possibility of resurrection and transformation from that which is not into that which is and ever shall be.

The physical elements of a wafer of bread and a cup of wine are made up of molecules and atoms and each atom has a nucleus. At the center of each nucleus is a narrow opening and within that opening is contained the whole of the Kingdom. Contrary to popular belief, the Kingdom of Heaven is not 'out there'. The Kingdom of Heaven dwells within. When the priest - the one consecrated and sanctified by God for the role of administering the Eucharist - celebrates the Mass, each nucleus within each atom of the elements begins a gyroscopic spin. They spin faster and faster until rings upon rings of pure light are created. Each atom is deified and the nucleus within each atom turns and faces God-ward. A channel of pure light anoints each nucleus and blesses it until it assumes the exact cellular makeup of Our Lord and Savior. For when Christ walked on the earth, He was formed of earthly matter and substance, while at the same time He remained divine. Every cell of His body was charged with the substance of eternity. Prior to His crucifixion He was one of us. He was effectively God made man - Three-in-One plus one - and as such He was communing osmotically with the Divine at all times. During His earthly life, His divinity flowed out towards the broken, the diseased and the possessed. But at the moment of Christ's death, His heart exploded and at the same time imploded into the center of all that is and into the purest of light, creating the possibility of divinity among that which is mortal and finite. A gate was effectively flung open which allowed humankind to attain the possibility of eternity. It was this that rocked the earth and had the result of breaking open the tombs, shaking the planet on its axis, blinding the shining stars, quenching the moon and dulling the sun. Christ's resurrected body thus remains forever imprinted within the collective cellular structure. This creates the possibility of transubstantiation and the possibility of divinity and of sanctity for those who would strive for such a state and those who would will such a state through their love of Christ.

It is this memory of His divine make-up within the collective material field that is reinstated at the moment of consecration. The essential memory of Him is plucked from all matter and is able to be manifested in the actuality of His Blessed Body once more. The beating heart of Christ resonates within a humble wafer and is transformed. This serves to create light and a doorway, which allows that which is of heaven into this finite world.

The practice of contemplation before the consecrated Host similarly allows a doorway through which the Infinite can break into in the dullness of the finite world and enter the worldly consciousness. The mystery of prayer before Exposition of the Host has the potential of affording great blessing to those who choose to practice it. Such prayer provides spiritual sustenance to the soul and the graces afforded are manifold. Prayer before Exposition is a practice not favored by all, but just because something cannot be tangibly 'felt', does not take away its essential spiritual meaning and validity. During such prayer one effectively places oneself before a doorway through which the soul is able to be anointed by the Divine. This brings healing to oneself and those for whom one prays. It essentially provides a crack in the world of finite things, allowing the admission of that which is of eternity. Here one places oneself on the radial pulse connected to the heart of the Divine. As such one receives the ability to channel grace throughout one's finite consciousness, scattering light and helping to bring healing to the fallen world.

Christ's earthly death and subsequent resurrection also heralded an outpouring of the Holy Spirit upon all believers - the living manifestation of the resurrected Christ. This gift of profound blessing continues to act catalytically today and enables Christian believers to live their spiritual lives in fullness.

At the time of the first believers, the promised gift of the Holy Spirit was fulfilled on the day of Pentecost when: 'Suddenly there came from the sky what sounded like a strong, driving wind, a noise which filled the whole house where they were sitting. And there appeared to them flames like tongues of fire distributed among them and coming to rest on each one. They were all filled with the Holy Spirit and began to talk in other tongues, as the Spirit gave them power of utterance.'[2] This profound event effectively transformed a group of tremulous, rather cowardly individuals into the driving force that was destined to become the root of the Christian Church.

The process by which the Holy Spirit enters the life of the individual occurs by an osmotic fusion of sorts. By virtue of relinquishment of the self to Christ, a space is formed within the heart, into which the Holy Spirit is able to enter and thereafter becomes an empowering catalyst. This process brings about a binding together of that which is divine, with that which is of the earth. This is a phenomenon that can only fully take place in a state of complete abandonment to God. In other words, the egotistical self needs to get completely out of the way, in order for Christ to fully occupy the heart. If the will remains doggedly in situ this has the effect of putting the brakes on the Holy Spirit's ability to work as He should. Thus the individual needs to die entirely in terms of the ego, in order that the lifeblood of Christ may course through the inner life and fully actualize all that the person was originally created to be. One may perhaps wonder why this could not happen in the first place and why all of the struggle is necessary. Would it not be simpler if everyone were able to be born into an instant utopia of perfect and harmonious existence, where one is truly oneself from the start? Well if this were to happen it would defeat the whole object of free will in the context of the earthly journey. In order for everything to unfold with absolute validity, each person needs the opportunity to find his or her way back to God of their own volition.

10.

THE HIDDEN TREASURE

Way back in the garden of Eden, all seemed well for Adam and Eve. Thus far their lives had consisted of an halcyon existence of harmonious living with their fellow creatures. They were subservient to God, but at the same time they were cherished by Him. And such subservience does not denote a state of inferiority at all. Indeed, if one is completely loved, one gains all things. But, as their story unfolded, the serpent lured Eve to eat the fruit of the forbidden tree in the garden - a fruit capable of instilling god-like qualities and status.[1] It was here that the 'I' of the ego first began to rear its ugly head - the key to all future human problems, difficulties and pain. This volatile element of the human condition, when unchecked, has the potential to spread through the consciousness like a forest fire. It has the capacity to infiltrate every area of people's lives, affecting in a myriad of different ways the multiplicity of the choices made on a daily basis. Its calling card is an all-consuming thirst for power and self-aggrandizement. In other words, where the ego rules, all that is divine is completely edged out. It also has the ability to asphyxiate the embryo of the true self - which lies dormant within the human heart. Darkness was thus permitted its first entry into the collective human consciousness - which would eventually give rise to terminal blockages that would serve to stifle the force of love. As a result the enlivening and healing energy of love began to be curtailed from reaching those who were starving emotionally and spiritually. Indeed, at the present time, the human race can be said to be on a perilous, slippery slope - careering relentlessly towards a metaphorical myocardial infarction. Gangrenous outcrops of darkness steadily contaminate the purity of the collective human soul. Humankind now consists of a series of hierarchic pecking orders, where rank egotism swamps and suffocates that which is life-giving and enlivening. Within the human race, on an individual level, there exist countless formative scenarios where love is denied or withheld for one reason or another. The resulting chain of negativity brings the fruit of destruction in terms of self, relationships and society in general. The only possible remedy is a steady saturation of unconditional loving kindness, but sadly there are few in today's spiritually and emotionally defunct society who are qualified to give the input of such remedial healing. And at the very center of the inherent darkness dwells a malevolent undercurrent that is continually striving to manipulate human brokenness in a negatively destructive way. At its root is an energy of pure evil that manifests itself in various guises in its virulent hatred of love, righteousness and truth. This putrid, stinking force is spreading insidiously throughout the human race, serving to mar, maim and injure bodies and minds. But thankfully, this is not the end of the story. Love, with all of its boundlessness and beauty, patiently waits in the wings for the opportunity to heal and make whole. While the human race can be said to be presently very far from liberation and true freedom, the good news is that there is still potential to change and there is still hope.

At the very center of each human soul dwells a 'pearl of great price'.[2] The potentiality and possibility of pure love waits in the hush of the soul center, in readiness to radiate outwards and to infuse the authentic self. When harnessed correctly, this love has the potential to bring into being that which is true and real in the individual. This love has great healing power and profound creativity. All that is lovely and wonderful on the earth has its origin in love, and each one of us, without exception, has been created by God for the purpose of receiving that love. Love is the sole reason for our being on the earth. God, the Creator, waits in endless longing to lavish His love upon us and for us to love Him in return. And as a byproduct of this two way exchange, He desires us to love ourselves and others in the same way. Where there is poverty of any sort - be it material, physical, emotional or spiritual - the poorer and weaker elements of human nature naturally yearn for an infilling of that which is richer and stronger. The ideal is for the individual soul to operate at his or her full potential and this will only prove possible when each soul has been filled to the brim with the restoring, healing energy of love. If such a situation existed on a worldwide scale, there would be no darkness anymore and every living thing would be saturated with the light of divine love.

The ultimate solution to all human problems and difficulties is for love and light to be released into individual lives and corporate situations. And the only way for this to begin to happen is by bringing about primary changes in the lives of individuals. Such changes may only be initiated by concentrating on that which is true and good and positive. The world can only become a better place if individuals strive to take responsibility for their own particular corner. If small individual changes for the better were to take place, this would potentially bring about a massive positive shift in the world as a whole. The challenge is to learn to work collectively in order to create and store up that most abiding of sustaining foods - the energy of pure love. Healing of the heart of humanity ultimately lies in drawing forth the same nature and quality of love that once served to break the heart of its Creator.

The love that initially existed in unformed souls at the beginning of time was innocent and pure and lacked an essential element. It was a docile, one-dimensional love - a love that had not yet been tested to its limits. The love that Almighty God wishes to bring to birth in each soul and collectively throughout the human race is a self-perpetuating, unconditional and self-giving love. Suffering often acts as the grit in the oyster shell of the heart of individuals - a concept once famously described by the Christian author and apologetic C. S. Lewis as: 'His megaphone to rouse a deaf world'.[3] But suffering is not inflicted on humankind by a despotic and uncaring God as many petulantly assert. All suffering is self-inflicted by humankind by virtue of the extreme poverty of its collective heart. Suffering is the 'wake-up call' to a spiritually slumbering humanity that is presently walking on a potential minefield of self-destruction.

Everywhere one cares to look are the symptoms of the heart sickness of humankind - disease, famine and disorders of the natural world culminating in various disasters that cause wreckage of human lives. In the world there exists a spiritual enemy whose one aim is to thwart and frustrate the human quest for eternal peace and happiness. This insidious force deliberately throws into the path of individual souls various 'spanners in the works', designed to pull them off course and away from their true and rightful destiny. The malign element behind this attack is fully aware that in our human state we become that which we desire. If we therefore show signs of changing course towards the direction of love and truth, the attack is intensified accordingly. The human race thus finds itself tempted by the lure of glittering worldly prizes, which seem to possess the potential of satisfying its unnamed hunger. We are led to wander down countless blind alleys and expend such energy and effort that we end up exhausted and wracked with frustration and disappointment. And still we feel ourselves to be a million miles away from achieving the fulfillment that we so ardently desire. Some of the goals pursued appear relatively innocuous - the aforementioned and apparently harmless ambitions of career and wealth, which in fact have the potential to wound us greatly if they are worshiped and adulated in an excessive way. These aspirations, while lauded and applauded by our peers, ultimately lead to disappointing cul-de-sacs of barren emptiness. Some of us fall by the wayside having succumbed to the tantalizing pull of more damaging life choices. These deadly traps and snares lie in wait, apparently offering instant comfort and sustenance, but again turn out to be veritable minefields which contain the potential to obscure the way to truth altogether. If so tempted, the hapless soul finds him or herself floundering in an all-consuming quicksand.

Even within their most intimate relationships many people find themselves existing on an essentially superficial level. The result of such shallow living is a profound inner emptiness. Thus we find, on examining our lives at the end of the day, that our journeys have somehow become diminished to a mere paddling in the shallow waters of inconsequential meaninglessness. It is this trough of disillusionment that often serves to light the touchpaper of the beginnings of dramatic change. For it is at times of extreme weakness and despair that we at last consent for our fractious tears to be wiped away by the source of love. And this first touch of healing has the effect of mobilizing us out of our spiritual torpor and propelling us forward into the light of eternity. It marks the beginning of our awakening from a state of mortality to that of everlasting life. At last we begin to discover that we are descended from the parentage of an unconditional love so great that it has endured death on our behalf. Once the indwelling divine spark has thus been kindled into a flame, there is a corresponding explosion of new life within our hearts. The stagnant pools of our ego-dominated personalities begin to fill to the brim with fresh, vibrant, sparkling new water. The irrigating source is an eternal spring which lies in the very apex of our souls. A stream of abundant life proceeds to flow unrestrainedly to every corner of our beings, leaving a trail of new blossom in its wake. We begin to realize that, thus far in our lives, we have been hypnotized and controlled by the cloying influence of the finite world. It is with liberating relief, therefore, that we at last begin to become cognizant of the authenticity of who we really are.

11.

TRUE PRAYER (1)

In the early days of brand new conversion, the novice believer makes a life changing decision to invite Christ in, and there takes place a change of heart or metanoia. In some cases this step is triggered by an evangelical gathering where the message of truth is heard as if for the first time. In the powerfully fervent atmosphere of such a meeting, the individual often becomes intensely aware of a deep emptiness and longing within the heart. Bathed in the light of newly charged belief, the convert might well imagine that a 'fait accompli' has taken place and that from now on life will be all plain sailing. It is indeed true that the all-important step has been taken, but thereafter further commitment will need to be reasserted each and every day of one's life. One will need constantly to ask oneself whether the leaven of faith and belief is present throughout one's life, or whether it is restricted to certain parts only. The commitment to Christ and His Kingship must be apparent in each and every facet of one's existence, as this is the only way to true liberation and freedom. One's new belief means that, when faced with life's inherent problems, one's automatic knee jerk reaction henceforward will be to turn God-ward. This whole process is perhaps similar to the concept of a novice pilot being taught to do the opposite of what comes naturally when in the grip of a dangerous spin. It is exactly the same in the

True Prayer (1)

context of the Christian faith, in the sense that a total free-fall abandonment to God is necessary when negotiating problems along the way. The very act of relinquishment and the concept of doing nothing of one's own volition will then have the positive effect of continually re-setting the rudder of one's life towards God. This whole concept proves notoriously difficult for many people - the reason being that the human ego forms such an inextricable part of the basic human survival instinct. The ego, or the definitive 'I', comprises a series of inner safety mechanisms which fuel the human need for control and the resolve not to lose supremacy at any cost. But it is only by a separate 'dying' in each and every area of one's existence that one can ultimately hope to be transformed and raised to abundant life. A deliberate nailing of the ego to Christ's Cross is needful in order to lay the ground for the eventual resurrection of the true self. At the point of conversion, the latter is normally deeply buried and has no hope at all of being uncovered unless one submits, of one's own volition, to a crucifixion of the ego. This notoriously leaves one broken, derelict and useless in the world's eyes, but subsequently something wondrous will start to happen - the beginning of the birth of Christ within the soul center. His transforming power will then be set free to blaze a trail towards a hallowed place where one's life can truly begin in earnest - in a promised land of truth, peace, happiness and fulfillment. For it is our true and real selves that have been invited to the wedding feast and it is only in a state of complete authenticity that we will at last be permitted to gaze upon the Glory of Almighty God. This truth will continue to be revealed as we journey onwards into the light of eternity. But from this moment on, we need to be solicitous in providing an environment that will ensure the nurture of the burgeoning truth within us. It is essential therefore to begin to foster the beginnings of a genuine life of prayer, for it is only within such arable soil that the soul will properly be able to flourish and develop.

The aim of prayer is not to spend vast amounts of time with one's head in the clouds in a state of reclusive unsociability. Its key purpose is the rediscovery of the 'pearl of great price'[1] - the true and authentic self. To embark on an individual prayer journey simply requires putting aside a regular period each day for the purpose of stillness and reflection. The early morning is ideal - before the mind has had a chance to become overly cluttered with the minutiae of daily events. From the outset it is advisable to enlist the accompaniment of an experienced director of souls - someone who has traveled along the path of Christian prayer for some time. But it is equally important to remember that one's ultimate counselor and guide will always be Christ Himself, through the inspiration of the Holy Spirit.

During the early stages of prayer, the mind often persists in behaving like an errant child, constantly throwing up one distraction after another, seemingly intent on thwarting one's best efforts. As soon as one begins to pray, worries and concerns of every conceivable sort race into one's thinking, jostling for instant attention. Thus the consciousness takes on the resemblance of a muddy pool with numerous issues, that bear no relation at all to the task in hand, continually rising to the surface. In order to exert a measure of control over this frustrating phenomenon it is helpful to provide the mind with a focal point for the duration of the prayer. A visually orientated individual may find success in meditating before a lighted candle or a religious icon. If one is an 'ideas' person, ruminating on an evocative word, verse or sentence may prove fruitful. Still others are greatly helped by using the Rosary or the Jesus Prayer.[2] But one should always remember that every method of prayer serves merely as a doorway or route to the journey's end and should not be seen as the destination in itself.

The process of prayer can never be forced in any way and one should try not to place too much emphasis on the achievement of discernible 'results'. The old adage: 'pray as you can, not as you can't'[3] often proves to be sound advice in the early stages. Prayer, by definition, is all about dwelling in the present moment and is essentially concerned with receiving not achieving. This flies against the wind of the modern-day dictum that anything of any real value can only be elicited by extreme and exhausting effort. The practice of prayer on a regular basis will eventually begin to yield positive results, the most noticeable being that previously chaotic areas of one's life will start to assume an unprecedented and melodious harmony. But ultimately, the God that we seek cannot be encompassed by worldly ideas and concepts and from the outset it will be necessary to let go of all preconceived notions about His essential identity. Indeed, any attempt to try to contain God using worldly comparisons and yardsticks will result in veering in the wrong direction entirely. But the 'scaffolding' of the familiar and the known often proves useful in the early stages of the prayer journey.

St Teresa of Avila once described prayer as: 'a friendly intercourse and frequent solitary conversation with Him who, as we know, loves us'.[4] Here, the saint referred to mental prayer - the practice of engaging the intellect in order to facilitate a path to inner silence. This proves an excellent starting point, for it is within our thoughts that we are most immediately present to all that we are as human beings. But once a modicum of stillness has been achieved at mind level, one should immediately seek to progress to the next stage - the descent towards the deepest heart. During my own lifetime on the earth, first as a layman and later as an ordained Anglican priest, my own preferred method of prayer was that of contemplation. This is perhaps best defined as a wordless conversation with the Almighty at the level of the heart. But the concept of stepping away from the perceived safety of the conscious mind often proves a difficult prospect for the intellectual individual, whose dependence on thinking and reasoning is deeply ingrained. This is why Christ said: 'whoever does not accept the kingdom of God like a child will never enter it'.[5] Our Lord was referring to the necessity of spiritual simplicity and the fact that too much 'baggage' in the material and intellectual sense can effectively douse the delicate flame of prayer completely. But even if one is intellectual in nature and even if one is burdened by great material riches one can still become a spiritual child. The key to the attainment of a state of spiritual simplicity can be summed up in one word - abandonment. For it is only when one surrenders completely to God with absolute and childlike trust that one can begin to receive all that He wishes to give to us. The paradox of the simplicity and complexity of prayer is succinctly described in the oft-quoted and beautiful exchange between the Blessed Cure D'Ars and a simple peasant. The latter, in an attempt to convey the nature of his prayer journey to his pastor confided: 'I say nothing to him - I look at him - and he looks at me.'[6] This profound statement succeeds in capturing the very essence of contemplative prayer in a proverbial nutshell.

The early stages of prayer may perhaps be compared to the construction of a jigsaw, in that it is relatively easy to slot into place the easily identifiable pieces of the outer edge. But then one is inevitably faced with the yawning space that exists in the middle. It is here that all pet theories about the essential identity of God begin rapidly to deflate. Here one finds oneself plunging into an endless sea of non-understanding, where all attempts at independent swimming prove absolutely fruitless. At this perplexing juncture, many individuals give up on the idea of prayer altogether and return with a measure of some relief to the instant gratification of the world. But if such a person were to just sit tight and resolve to stay the distance, the answers that they seek may prove closer and more accessible than they imagine. If one is fortunate enough to have on board the guidance of a wise spiritual director, such periods of barrenness will normally elicit reassurance that all is well, even when the opposite appears to be the case. One will be advised of the necessity to prepare oneself for what may prove to be a lengthy period of apparently fruitless spiritual non-activity. In other words, one should become accustomed to the practice of 'floating' prayerfully, for as long as is necessary, upon the vast ineffable sea that is eternity. But although it may feel at this point that nothing important is happening, much will be in progress at an imperceptible and immeasurable level. For it is true to say that worldly parameters and comparisons cannot be applied to the spiritual life.

In the context of prayer, there is no way of achieving the modern-day penchant for instant results. In God's own time and own way, one will eventually receive a barely discernible but gentle invitation to move forward and when this happens it will be quite unmistakable and obvious. Such an experience proved true in the life of the prophet Elijah. Following a lengthy period of severe testing on a personal level, he eventually discovered the immediacy of God's presence within a 'still small voice'[7] that only his state of exhausted vulnerability enabled him to perceive. The necessity of periods of barrenness in prayer to facilitate inner growth has been recognized by spiritual masters for centuries. Such times of trial are indicative of the fact that the Author of love is gently beginning to ease the soul away from the spiritual nursery slopes towards the more rarified atmosphere of higher ground. A fine-tuning of previously dormant spiritual ears is in progress that will ultimately allow the perception of the subtle, less easily discernible music of the heavens. In other words, the soul is in the process of being invited to enter the 'narrow gate' referred to in the Gospels.[8]

There are many pilgrims who react to the aridity of harsh spiritual trials by panicking completely and making an instant U-turn back to a former, seemingly less demanding level of the journey. Here they proceed to close their spiritual ears and commence an interminable, self-imposed process of 'treading water', thus rendering them stationary in terms of further progress. The root of the problem often proves to be that they have caught a disconcerting glimpse of the vast 'nothing-ness' of God and this has planted fear at a certain level. Their discomfiting perception sometimes has the knock-on effect of triggering a subconscious 'work to rule' in terms of discovering more about God. From the spiritual direction point of view, there is absolutely nothing that one can do to help, as ultimately everyone is required to face the reality and imperceptibility of their Creator alone. But at the same time, it is important not to be overly critical, as it may be that such an individual has simply absorbed, for the time being, as much light and truth as they can essentially bear. Almighty God is infinitely patient with regard to the rate at which each soul handles spiritual growth. Such tremulous pilgrims often proceed to carry out admirable 'hands-on' work for Christ in a worldly context, while at the same time voluntarily electing to remain in the apparent safety of prayer's foothills. But the more intrepid and ardent pilgrim possesses an unrelenting and burning desire to press ever onward towards higher ground, in a quest to discover the way that is found by the few. This is the path that will eventually lead to the creation of a whole new person - a twenty-four carat version of oneself that is indelibly shot through with the mark of the Divine.

12.

TRUE PRAYER (2)

In the Gospels, we are given an illustrative example of two quintessential paths of prayer as depicted in the lives of two sisters: Martha and Mary.[1] Mary is presented as a 'textbook' contemplative who delights in spending lengthy periods of silent adoration at the feet of her Lord, while her sibling Martha busies herself in a never-ending frenzy of impeccable doting service. During the account, we are told that Martha eventually gives way to a jealous diatribe during which she condemns her sister's apparent laziness. She at once receives a gentle rebuke from Our Lord who infers that Mary's silence pleases Him more than her own incessant buzz of activity. The interminable battle of silence versus activity, in the context of the spiritual life, proves no different today. 'Active' Christians continue to exhibit impatience towards their more reflective peers, who outwardly appear to be achieving very little in terms of Christian service. The former consider that time on the earth is more usefully spent in physically helping others in the Name of Christ. But the aforementioned Gospel passage aims to convey that the prayer journey should ideally contain a balanced mixture of both active and contemplative elements. Our Lord Himself was a prime example of this, in that His earthly ministry was spent in constant bone-grinding self-giving, while His nights remained shrouded in a mystery of contemplative seclusion at the feet of His Heavenly Father. Both aspects proved to be completely interdependent and indivisible from the other. Our Lord's days of tireless ministry were so effective because He took the time to recharge His spiritual batteries during His nightly mountain-top sojourns. And the unceasing nature of His daily ministry gave substance to His nocturnal prayer of contemplation and adoration. But there are some souls whose spiritual vocation is purely contemplative and for whom to remain constantly at God's feet in worship and adoration is their absolute and only calling. I refer here to those who are committed to monastic vows in religious orders or those who choose to follow a similar path in the world in the context of their normal daily lives. There are also individuals whose life situations and personal circumstances dictate that the only possible way that they are able to express their love of God is through stillness, prayer and intercession. All such souls are specifically called by God to be beacons of light and channels of spiritual power within our troubled world. Their hidden inner work has a powerful catalytic effect on the collective human consciousness, the results of which will not become fully apparent until we all reach the greater life. Such individuals should therefore not be criticized for their apparent inactivity by their seemingly more 'productive' brothers and sisters, as they are in the process of providing an essential spiritual back-up for the active ministry of the Church as a whole. As such they exist on the front line in the battle between darkness and light. We all need to work together in harmony, and precious energy should not be constantly wasted in casting aspersions or in criticism of one another. Instead we should go out of our way to encourage, support and celebrate the unique giftedness of each one of us. As St Paul reminds us in his letter to the Romans: 'just as in a single human body there are many limbs and organs, all with different functions, so we who are united with Christ, though many, form one body, and belong to one another as its limbs and organs. Let us use the different gifts allotted to each of us by God's grace - - -.'[2]

At the very beginning of the Christian prayer journey we effectively place ourselves into the hands of a Master Sculptor. We give God permission to fashion our souls back to their original blueprint, which in turn will reveal the essential truth of our beings. In this context, the medium of silence is an enabling catalyst in the life of prayer - a concept that can often prove challenging for those who are accustomed to the heaving maelstrom of modern day existence. But in order to attune oneself to the delicate mysteries of the Spirit, one needs to wean oneself away from undue dependence on endless communication and frantic activity. For it is only before the revelatory mirror of silence that one can really begin to perceive one's true identity in Christ and can hope to uncover the myriad of treasures that are hidden in the depths of one's being. Within the medium of silence we expose our souls to the light of God's presence and travel further towards the goal of becoming authentic human beings. Those, in other words, who will witness to the Kingdom of God, not especially by doing but by being - in the context of whatever situation we find ourselves at any particular time.

The basic reason that silence presents an uneasy and uncomfortable medium to some people is that its searching spotlight has a tendency to bring to light unresolved and painful issues from the past. I have shared elsewhere about the nature of my own childhood wounds, which remained pressed down and buried at a subconscious level until I reached adulthood. The deliberate seeking of the silent space of an organized retreat may help to facilitate the rediscovery of the lost child within oneself. In such a situation one will be able to avail oneself of long stretches of uninterrupted and focused reflection, away from the vicissitudes and pressures of one's normal daily life. This will often serve to bring about full realization of one's own inner woundedness and need for healing. One will also have recourse to the guidance and support of a retreat director who will be experienced in spiritual accompaniment. Embarkation on a retreat journey for the first time will inevitably engender a modicum of hesitation, due to the fear of the unknown. The prospect of deliberately placing oneself in a position of naked vulnerability before the power and mystery of God may at first prove extremely daunting. However, it will take much time, prayer and perhaps many more periods of retreat before one eventually reaches the position of uncovering one's true identity in Christ. This will come hand in hand with the discovery of one's 'raison d'être' or soul-purpose - for it is not by chance that we are born on the earth and each of us has a predestined task to fulfil. The brilliant Christian writer and apologetic C. S. Lewis described the transformative process of the soul thus: 'We are to be re-made. All the rabbit in us is to disappear - the worried, conscientious, ethical rabbit as well as the cowardly and sensual rabbit. We shall bleed and squeal as the handfuls of fur come out; and then, surprisingly, we shall find underneath it all a thing we have never yet imagined: a real Man, an ageless god, a son of God, strong, radiant, wise, beautiful, and drenched in joy.'[3]

Any progress made on the path towards communion with God is largely imperceptible to one's own self and is never heralded by a great emotional song and dance. Indeed, it is important, in the context of prayer, not to place too much emphasis on transient emotions and feelings. God may well provide tangible favors at the very start of the journey, but as time goes on such encouragements will normally only occur as an occasional gift. The prophet Jeremiah drew specific reference to the unreliability of the emotions in his telling statement: 'The heart is deceitful above any other thing, desperately sick; who can fathom it?'[4] One should thus do one's best to move away from undue dependence on emotions, because ultimately they will prove immaterial and unnecessary. All that is needful is the faith that Christ is always with us, whether we are able to perceive it tangibly or not. But the very act of moving closer to God requires us to play our own part in striving to open our hearts more fully to the love that He wishes to give us. There are some individuals who find this process difficult due to wounds arising from the past. I myself, as a result of my childhood traumas, developed a tendency to erect internal protective barriers, which resulted in difficulty in receiving and giving love during my earthly life. A lot of people did love me and often told me so, but I was unable properly to receive their love or to respond in kind, due to my own inner woundedness. I had effectively built a wall around my heart, as is so often the case when one has been deeply hurt as a child. In all areas of faith I was aware of what essentially mattered intellectually, but emotionally everything persisted in remaining somewhat nebulous and hazy. In my case, all personal experience relating to the giving and receiving of love tended to take place on a purely mystical level. This emotionally redundant state persisted right to the end of my lifetime on earth. But when I eventually passed to the greater life and my early wounds were fully healed, it was as if the curtains finally parted and I was at last able to experience tangible emotion for the first time. This gift proved all the greater due to my former barren existence behind those numbing protective walls. So to those whose state of inner woundedness mirrors my own, I would say - try to remain steady in the essential faith of the reality of Christ's love - a love that was undeniably proven by the fact that Our Lord died for each one of us individually on the Cross. One should strive to keep this precious nugget of knowledge uppermost in one's mind and heart at all times, as it constitutes the unchanging cornerstone of the Christian faith - the immutable fact that God loves each one of us unconditionally. It is important to assert the remembrance of this a thousand times each day, so that one always knows it without doubt at mind level, even if one is unable presently to process it and to feel it tangibly within one's heart.

The ultimate aim of prayer is union with Almighty God and in order to reach this goal, one essentially needs to become as nothing. Not in the sense of diminishment at all, but in the actualization of one's own true being and the jettisoning of all that is worldly. For it is only by fully realizing and accepting that of oneself one is nothing, that one can ever hope to become united with the Divine. The process towards union with God begins at the point of conversion, at which time a fundamental change occurs within the heart. This concept was famously observed by John Wesley in his description of the phenomenon of his heart being 'strangely warmed'.[5] This was indeed an accurate allegory, as the state of conversion has the effect of causing the divine nucleus within the heart to burst into a small flame. But while the concepts of abandonment, self-forgetfulness and relinquishment are of paramount importance in the spiritual life, one also needs at the same time to remain 'grounded' in one's essential state of humanity. If, during one's earthly span, one were to deny and reject the human state entirely in order to focus solely on the spiritual, this would serve to bring about alienation from our non-believing fellows. We would thus lose all common ground with those to whom we should be aiming to impart a positive spiritual message.

In order to reach the state of divine union, the 'I' of the ego needs be purged of all that is selfish and gross - a process that takes place over a very long period of time and is often not complete at the point of death. There have been exceptions however. The Blessed Virgin Mary displayed no ego or 'I' from the moment of her birth. Hers was a soul of grace, perfect at its very conception. But in most cases, the soul only fully reaches a point of absolute surrender to the Divine once a total purgation of the human ego is complete. It is at this point that the flame within the heart springs into a greater light, which then has the knock-on effect of instilling an identical light within the exalted center of the mind. Then finally, the redeemed ego is transformed into the likeness of Christ. St Paul's words: 'I have been crucified with Christ: the life I now live is not my life, but the life which Christ lives in me,'[6] referred to the unitive state in the saint's own life. This statement was indicative of the fact that his human ego had become fully sublimated to God. In this exalted state, the emotions, the sexual urges and the base feelings of the ego become sanctified and completely surrendered to the Divine. When the moment of divine union is attained, the ego becomes divinized, while continuing to retain the memory of what it is to be human. The transformed ego then becomes capable of blessing others with divinized human love. As such it has the ability to act as a catalyst of light within the collective consciousness of humankind and is enabled, by virtue of its humanity, to mingle 'incognito' therein, while taking with it that which has become divine. This whole process could perhaps be compared with the concept in modern medical science of planting irradiated cells within the body to treat specific areas of cancerous tissue. The transformed mind becomes a 'thinking heart' and henceforward, all thoughts, concepts and decisions are sanctified. The transformed heart is saturated with the light of God and becomes a window through which divine light can flow in order to bless the world. And the newly lighted abdominal center - the dwelling place of the human ego - becomes a kernel of connection with all humanity. At this stage one has effectively become an ambassador for Christ in the world and a source of light, love and peace. In other words one has essentially become Christified, while at the same time remaining fully human. But union with Christ does not mean that one loses one's own essential personhood in any way, shape or form, but rather that one has been enabled to become a tool of wisdom and a catalyst for good within the collective consciousness of humankind.

As one moves nearer to the Godhead, a period of adjustment is necessary in order to become accustomed to the sheer brilliance of the light of God's Presence. At first the divine light may appear as a glittering darkness, due to its blinding intensity. But as one is gradually exposed to the light of God, measure by measure, the soul will begin to adapt, and the eyes of the heart will gradually be opened. The truth of one's own personhood will gradually be revealed by Christ's transforming light. The former shams and pretences of one's life on earth will be illuminated and one will be able to see the extent of one's own imperfections which, as mentioned earlier, can be an intensely painful process. The light of God thus acts as a gentle force, searching out and exposing the previously hidden places of our inner beings. This revelatory process can come as quite a shock for individuals who have previously existed in a state of veiled unawareness. Ultimately, it will prove necessary to become completely reconciled to our past demons, as only then will we be enabled to move forward as truly liberated people. The words of Christ: 'you will know the truth, and the truth will set you free,'[7] describes the process of inner transformation. Once the soul has been cleansed of all dross, it will then be able to look fully into the eyes of the Father for the first time and as such it will at last see the reflected beauty of its own true self. It will be able to embrace and 'own' its true identity as a son or daughter of the King and will know the purpose of its presence within our fractured world. For the ultimate destiny of each and every one of us is to play an essential part in the world's liberation and healing.

Spiritual growth, in the context of prayer, is a process that takes place gradually and imperceptibly. It is something that will not always be apparent to the person concerned and will normally be far more noticeable to those looking on - those who know the person well. The fact that such inner growth has occurred is often revealed by a new and unprecedented ability to respond with greater aplomb to life's vicissitudes, tests and challenges. Quite suddenly, one begins to display the presence of greater inner strength and toughness of character that was most definitely not there before. The cause of such positive changes is the development of new 'spiritual muscles' which have a ripple effect throughout the whole personality. It is also true to say that one area cannot grow without it affecting every other aspect of one's being.

But the most important catalyst to inner maturity is the love that one receives from Almighty God during contemplative prayer. This gift of unreserved and unconditional acceptance has the effect of transmuting the deepest aspects of one's being. It has the end result that one gradually becomes stronger in every way, due to a new self-acceptance of every facet of oneself - 'warts and all'. It marks the beginning of self-love - though not in the egoistical sense at all, but in the cherishing of every nuance of one's own personhood, simply because God loved us first. This inner upbuilding is one of the most important products of contemplative prayer. When exposed to the light of God's gracious Presence, one begins slowly to unfurl the formerly tightly bound petals of one's inner being, with the end result that one finally begins to blossom into full humanity. Through the same process, one also begins to reflect God's light within one's individual life situation. Each area of one's life thus becomes filtered through the refraction of the window of the Divine. This does not mean that life will become easier in any sense, nor does it mean that all of our human problems will instantly go away. It simply means that we will begin to see life from a completely different perspective and that our vision will henceforward be bathed in the light of God. In other words, while on the earth, we will truly have become full citizens of Heaven.

As we have already discussed, at the very start of the contemplative journey one's inner life normally consists of a jumbled hotchpotch of unhealed material. In most cases, a myriad of issues and situations within the past remain unresolved and unhealed. We have already touched upon the concept of deliberate retreat in helping one to become aware of one's inner woundedness. But in the context of daily life, there are also other tools of which one may avail oneself in the redemptive spiritual journey of inner healing. These are the tried and tested 'man-made' methods of psychotherapy and counseling. Ultimately it will only be by the prayer of contemplation that one will be able to reach the state necessary to allow union with Almighty God. But having said this, the processes of psychotherapy and counseling are eminently useful in giving much needed support to those traveling upon the painful path of inner healing. This may essentially be a long and a difficult process. Overall, there needs to be a complete 'handed-over-ness' to God on every level at all times, until eventually the unifying experience with Almighty God is able to take place within the heart. For it is primarily within the heart that the initial interchange takes place and it is here that the soul begins to become one with Him: 'who is, who was, and who is to come'.[8] Consider the words: 'Blessed are those whose hearts are pure; they shall see God'.[9] The 'seeing' referred to in this passage could also be described as a 'knowing.' The unitive process is an emotive issue as it is the pinnacle of all that we are striving for within the context of our individual inner journeys. But one should also consider the vulnerability of God when, in total purity and love, He seeks to reach forth to touch and to anoint an individual soul. In so doing He sends forth waves of pure, pure love and brings about the deepest healing possible within the incarnate state. And at the same time, in our human frailty and poverty, we are invited to reach out to anoint our Creator with the paltry widow's mite of the love that exists in our own hearts.

13.

THE SPIRIT FILLED LIFE

Prior to His death on the Cross, Our Lord made the following promise: 'The advocate, the Holy Spirit whom the Father will send in my name, will teach you everything and remind you of all that I have told you.'[1] This blessing was destined to become available to all believers following Christ's Ascension and continues to rest upon individual petition. Our Lord specifically states: 'Ask, and you will receive; seek, and you will find; knock, and the door will be opened to you. For everyone who asks receives, those who seek find, and to those who knock, the door will be opened.'[2]

The Holy Spirit is an intrinsic part of Almighty God. He is the Spirit of Jesus Christ and as such He has the catalytic potential to bring about the living of the Christian life in all its fullness. But He will never presume to manifest Himself of His own volition and He will always wait for the specific invitation of the individual concerned. Before this glorious benediction is able to be endowed, there may be issues that first need to be addressed. Perhaps one has prayed for this empowering gift for some time, but as yet one's prayer has not been answered. In such a case, it may be necessary to undertake what is known as an 'examination of conscience'. This is a procedure that should be carried out with regularity and is something to be especially encouraged before embarking on a period of personal retreat. It is a concept that is perhaps more familiar within Roman Catholic and High Anglican persuasions and simply means going through one's life with a fine toothcomb, to determine whether there are factors that are preventing the liberation and release of the Holy Spirit into each and every part of one's life. An examination of conscience is best executed under the watchful eye of a trusted spiritual guide. In order to proceed, one should ideally split up one's life up into equal periods of time. Within these sections, one should ask oneself whether there is any matter that has never properly been given closure. In St Matthew's gospel Our Lord states: 'Anyone who nurses anger against his brother must be brought to justice. Whoever calls his brother "good for nothing" deserves the sentence of the court; whoever calls him "fool" deserves hellfire. So if you are presenting your gift at the altar and suddenly remember that your brother has a grievance against you, leave your gift where it is before the altar. First go and make your peace with your brother; then come back and offer your gift.'[3] In the general sense, one may be aware of being 'squeaky clean' in certain areas of one's life and concurrently floundering in others. In the management of one's spiritual journey, it is necessary to keep each and every part of one's life within the air of pure prayer at the same time. If any aspect is neglected and falls to the floor, this will serve to distract attention and solicitude from another, causing one's proverbial ship to begin to sink. The skill of perpetually keeping the whole of our lives within the light of prayer is something that can never be achieved by an act of human will. It can only come about by abandoning one's self in totality to Almighty God on a moment by moment basis. Only after many years of practice does this mindset become a perpetual reality and something that one no longer needs to think about at all. The powerful words of the book of Revelation express Christ's invitation to the soul: 'Here I stand knocking at the door; if anyone hears my voice and opens the door, I will come in and he and I will eat together.'[4]

Christ constantly requests admittance to each and every area of our lives, but He would never presume to barge in unannounced like some sort of an overbearing parent. He always requires prior invitation in each case, and we ourselves are ultimately in control as to how much of Christ's light and Christ's Spirit dwell within us at any particular time. Only after a painstaking examination of one's life will one be able to discern and clear up any prevailing problems. Then one will at last be free to echo the words of the beautiful ancient hymn: 'Come, Holy Ghost, our souls inspire, and lighten with celestial fire.'[5]

There are some Christians who persist in the belief that the Holy Spirit is an archaic element belonging to New Testament times, asserting that this is an aspect of the Christian faith now outdated and unnecessary - an opinion, incidentally, that is often rooted in the individual's need for totalitarian inner control. This mindset is based on the perception that the Spirit is something 'dangerous' and 'risky', which potentially challenges one's habitual 'go it alone' lifestyle. But many believers firmly maintain that the gift of the Holy Spirit is vitally necessary in order to live the Christian life in fullness. Again, the more conservative believers regard this view with some suspicion and have a tendency to relegate all charismatic phenomena to a category of pure emotionalism. But one could perhaps compare the Spirit-less Christian existence as akin to being gifted a brand new motor car which one then laboriously insists on pushing from place to place. Eventually, one may find oneself in the humbling position of being overtaken by a speedier vehicle, and then being greeted at one's destination with the question: 'Dear friend - have you never heard of petrol?' This analogy highlights the essential and empowering presence of the Holy Spirit in living the Christian life - the element that lights up one's existence with glorious and transcendent power.

In the course of my own earthly Christian journey, I knew of many 'closet' charismatic believers who were forced to keep quiet about the enlivening element of the Holy Spirit in their lives, in order not to rock the boat too vehemently within their own congregations. This was mainly due to an aversion among their fellows to the gift of glossolalia, or speaking in tongues - a phenomenon that is most visible in the charismatic sectors of the Church. This process involves a temporary bypassing of the conscious mind, which gives rise to an onrush of spontaneous utterance and praise of God. The language is commonly undecipherable by human means; but when it occurs in the setting of a Christian gathering, it is invariably accompanied by an interpretation by another member of the group. It then reveals itself to be an edifying and encouraging message which serves to upbuild other members. I myself used the gift of tongues constantly throughout my earthly Christian journey, having first come across the phenomenon at a charismatic meeting in London, where I was able to witness it first-hand. On this memorable occasion I found the Christian love and goodwill of the congregation greatly inspiring. Arriving home later that evening, I rather tentatively asked God that I too might receive the same blessing, but to my intense disappointment, nothing immediately happened as a result of my petition. However, the following morning, I awoke to find myself speaking spontaneously in a unknown tongue. This was accompanied by an intense feeling of warmth in the area of my heart, which then proceeded to spread through my whole body, until even my fingertips and toes glowed in an altogether pleasant way. That day, I was required to attend work as usual, but when I found myself alone I experimented to see whether or not the experience had been down to my imagination. I soon discovered that the amazing speech, with its accompanying sense of warmth and peace, came forth spontaneously and at will. As was my wont in all areas of non-understanding, I sat up well into the night reading extensively and voraciously scanning the Scriptures to find all documented evidence on the subject. All references seemed to state that the gift was related to the endowment of power within the Christian life, for the purpose of helping others.

In other words, it is not intended as a selfish manifestation, but is an empowering gift of ministry. I gradually began to experiment by silently using the gift during the administering of laying on of hands in counseling and healing situations and also during the ministry of deliverance. On all such occasions, I discovered that the Holy Spirit seemed able to bypass my own human frailty in order to address the need of the individual directly. I later received confirmation that I was using the gift correctly, when many people started to report back that my ministry had brought about positive changes in their lives.

The Spirit's infilling also brought about other dramatic changes in my life. For instance, I developed an ability to speak spontaneously at large gatherings without recourse to previously prepared notes. On such occasions, I would quite literally open my mouth and the inspired speech would begin to pour forth. I can honestly assert that I never had any idea beforehand what I was to say. I was often asked to speak on a particular topic and on such occasions I would simply keep the requested subject matter to the forefront of my mind and the Holy Spirit would do the rest.

Many Christians have a basic fear of the gift of tongues because it appears that one temporarily loses control of one's thoughts and one's words. But those who have experienced the phenomenon will verify that starting and stopping the flow of utterance is entirely within the control of the individual concerned. Some Christians may also have had the discomfiting experience of attending gatherings where the proceedings appear to fly out of control altogether. This type of display is entirely due to emotionally immature self-aggrandizement by a few key individuals, who seek to parade their gift in front of others as a form of pride. In other words this is simply an exhibition of childish showing off. The gift of tongues, as with any other spiritual ability, proves to be an extremely useful tool only if it is exercised correctly and with prudence.

In his letter to the Church at Corinth, St Paul gave a

detailed breakdown of the various gifts of the Holy Spirit saying: 'In each of us the Spirit is seen to be at work for some useful purpose.'[6] The latter is a very important point. The gift of the Holy Spirit is never bequeathed in order to increase one's own personal importance and standing among one's fellow Christians, but is given by God for the express purpose of upbuilding and edifying the Church as a whole. The gifts of the Spirit are manifold: 'One, through the Spirit, has the gift of wise speech, while another, by the power of the same Spirit, can put the deepest knowledge into words. Another, by the same Spirit, is granted faith; another, by the one Spirit, gifts of healing, and another miraculous powers; another has the gift of prophecy, and another the ability to distinguish true spirits from false; yet another has the gift of tongues of various kinds, and another the ability to interpret them. But all these gifts are the activity of one and the same Spirit, distributing them to each individual at will.'[7] In the same context St Paul goes on to address the competitive nature of his flock: 'There are varieties of gifts, but the same Spirit. There are varieties of service, but the same Lord. There are varieties of activity, but in all of them and in everyone the same God is active.'[8] There is much evidence to show that the early Church was prey to all too human traits of pride, competitiveness and exhibitionism in relation to the manifestation of spiritual gifts. But in perhaps the loveliest New Testament passage, St Paul specifically denounces all spiritual gifts entirely in favor of the greater gift of love. We are thus able to attain a very recognizable human picture of the early Church: a situation of jostling for prime position and of attempting to use the gifts of the Spirit for the purpose of supremacy and power. St Paul continually strives to bring his flock back to the all-important central focus: 'I may speak in tongues of men or of angels, but if I have no love, I am a sounding gong or a clanging cymbal. I may have the gift of prophecy and the knowledge of every hidden truth; I may have faith enough to move mountains; but if I have no love, I am nothing. I may give all I possess to the needy, I may give my body to be burnt, but if I have no love, I gain nothing by it. - - There are three things that last forever: faith, hope, and love; and the greatest of the three is love.'[9]

In the Scriptures, we initially encounter the Holy Spirit at the beginning of the book of Genesis, where we are told: 'the spirit of God hovered over the surface of the water'.[10] From the very start; the Holy Spirit is depicted as a catalytic, invisible factor carrying immense power. It is a basic fear of the concept of divine power that may sometimes prove to be a problem to individuals who reject the concept of the Holy Spirit altogether. Further confusion may come about by the fact that He cannot be seen or experienced by the immediate human senses and that His perception requires a spiritual dimension on the part of the receiver. The Holy Spirit of Old Testament times blazed His trail through the lives of the prophets, endowing ordinary individuals with super-human power, which served to dramatically change the course of human history and transformed those same individuals along the way. In the book of Isaiah, predictions are received of a coming Messiah. The very consciousness of the human race was thus being gradually prepared for a great event, which promised to bring the potential of healing to a world that had been shattered during the Fall.

In terms of the Christian life, the gift of the Holy Spirit can perhaps best be described as the 'icing on the cake' of the spiritual journey. Once one's past is fully reconciled to God and has been made new by the cleansing power of the Cross, one is then rendered free to claim the gift of the Spirit of God in one's own life. Henceforward the Spirit will work catalytically to enlighten the heart and will faithfully assist and aid in one's journey towards the ultimate safe harbor of the heavenly realms. Having said all of this, one should try not to analyze the Holy Spirit overmuch at the level of one's mind. In the earthly sense, He will eternally remain part of the mystery of Almighty God and as such can never truly be known within the limited scope of finite understanding. Solid immutable evidence that the Holy Spirit is positively present in an individual Christian life is always manifested by the presence of the fruits mentioned by St Paul in his letter to the Galatians. Namely those of: 'love, joy, peace, patience, kindness, goodness, fidelity, gentleness, and self-control'.[11] This is the spiritual 'barometer' that one may use to ascertain whether one is headed in the right direction. Thereafter it is necessary to invite the Holy Spirit into one's life on a daily basis in order to lay the foundation for eventual progression towards the ultimate state of divine union. As St Paul reminds us: 'we are being transformed into his likeness with ever-increasing glory, through the power of the Lord who is the Spirit'.[12] Or, as perhaps the greatest of all hymn writers Charles Wesley expounds: 'Finish then Thy new creation: pure and spotless let us be; let us see Thy great salvation, perfectly restored in Thee.'[13]

14.

PSYCHIC SENSITIVITY (1)

Psychic sensitivity, in the context of the Christian journey, has always been a much maligned area within the worldwide Church. But perhaps if the rampant critics were to spend a day attempting to handle such gifts themselves, they would begin to resonate to an entirely different tune. It is clear from the Scriptures that the incarnate Jesus Christ was acutely psychically sensitive. He possessed a wide spectrum of spiritual abilities, including insight into the secret workings of the human heart, accurate foreknowledge of future events and the ability to commune with those saints who had already passed through the veil of death. Our Lord's sensitivity eventually reached a climax in the Garden of Gethsemene,[1] when He allowed the collective agony of humankind to invade His soul center. The ensuing spiritual isolation that He experienced led to an inner crucifixion which shattered His heart completely. It would be interesting to observe the reaction of today's believers to Christ's spiritual gifts if He were to mingle incognito within the present day Church. Would He meet with negativity, hostility and suspicion from those who persist in limiting the collective growth of the Christian body by their damagingly narrow perception of belief?

Psychic sensitivity may be regarded in equal measures as both a blessing and a curse. On the positive side it is a state which undoubtedly brings untold spiritual blessings. But at the same time there is an accompanying underside of vulnerability in that one is also prey to assault from the more unsavory spiritual forces that exist within the psychic milieu. There is never a 'day off' from psychic sensitivity and one is called upon constantly to share in the suffering of souls, in this world and the next.

Most Christian sensitives begin to display accentuated levels of awareness during early childhood, while the full measure of psychic giftedness normally descends at around the age of puberty. I vividly remember the dawn of my own sensitivity as being heralded by a stark and sudden rise in clarity of perception. This was followed by violent propulsion into a strange new world that contained no guiding map or compass. By far the most alarming aspect of this state of affairs was a newly acquired ability to passively absorb the emotional states of those around me. I initially surmised that this never-ending stream of material had its origin within my own consciousness, which led to the fear that I may perhaps be heading for some type of mental breakdown. My anxiety was further compounded by a normal adolescent desire to be able to blend in as inconspicuously as possible with my peers. Thankfully, grace of insight into the true cause of my inner 'malaise' came relatively quickly. But much later in life, my ministry of spiritual direction was to bring me into contact with individuals whose introduction to the world of psychic sensitivity had not been as smooth as my own. I was then to hear countless distress stories of medical misdiagnoses of neuroses or worse, accompanied by reports of the indiscriminate prescribing of mind-numbing medications purported to be able to 'control' the sensitivity of the sufferer. It is true to say that medical practitioners who possess a working knowledge of psychical and spiritual matters are few and far between, with most proving dangerously inept when it comes to treating psychically sensitive individuals in an intelligent and holistic way. There is a strong need for positive and fruitful dialogue between the psychically astute in the Church and the medical profession, which would hopefully lead to an across the board recognition of the soul and the spirit as an intrinsic part of human reality.

In my own case, a simple everyday incident served to trigger the dawn of comprehension with regard to my psychic gifts. This came about one day when I was keeping company below stairs - a place that was infinitely more 'home' to me than the emotionally barren domain of the main house. My father burst in on the equable scene and proceeded to forcefully berate one of the kitchen maids over some minor misdemeanor or other. At the same time, I observed a corresponding elevation of emotional distress within my own consciousness. I knew at once that this was not simply a matter of coming out in sympathy with the person concerned and the realization began to dawn that I now possessed an ability to siphon away negative emotions from other people. There was little time for self-congratulation about this slick piece of psychic detective work, as I subsequently realized that I was completely unable to jettison the emotional burden, which clung, unmoving and limpet-like, to my innermost consciousness. I was thus forced to carry the distress until the said person had reached calmer waters. This incident was to be one among many. Thereafter I constantly found myself drawing negative material away from others in much the same way that a magnet attracts iron filings. Matters became infinitely worse when I was in a large group - for instance, at school, or in the marketplace setting of the heavily populated area in which we lived. On these occasions, all manner of diverse emotional material would rush towards my psyche and would proceed uncomfortably to take residence. I can recall countless instances of arriving home burdened with a wide variety of foreign material. It was my lack of essential control over these happenings that caused me the greatest anxiety at the time. Thankfully, however, assistance was close at hand in the form of an unpretentious spiritual 'guru' who happened to live on our premises. Incidentally, nothing occurs by accident and if our lives are committed to Almighty God, He, in His loving care and solicitude will provide us with helpmates along the way. The person to whom I refer was an elderly groundsman in the employ of my father. David was a placid, even-tempered individual who possessed a lifetime of experience in handling and managing his own psychic gifts. He was not only able to allay my fears, which by that time were threatening to spiral completely out of control, but he also willingly took on the role of unofficial spiritual guide. The new friendship proved very timely, as I was soon to be plunged into infinitely choppier spiritual waters. My gifts began to display a variety of new angles and tangents, including the discomfiting ability to be able to discern the presence of discarnate souls in the surrounding psychic milieu. These entities would make themselves known by moving inanimate objects in my immediate environment when I was alone at night. Initially I had no comprehension as to why all of this should be happening to me or indeed what I was expected to do about it. But with David's ongoing counsel and help, I eventually came to realize that I was being introduced to a lifetime of intercessory work on behalf of lost souls who were simply seeking the way home. A further element to my sensitivity included an ability to perceive spiritual emanations on a much larger scale. At the time, the wider world was experiencing the dawn of unrest which marked the beginnings of the Second World War. I found myself open to the seismic shock waves which were reverberating outwards from this concentrated kernel of human distress. By this time I was beginning to fear that I was forever destined to be a helpless passenger on a never-ending psychic switchback ride of indeterminate destination. It was the sense of complete powerlessness and lack of control over my gifts that proved to be the most distressing factor at the time. This state of affairs was further compounded by the various stresses and strains that are normally inherent in the life of a boy on the brink of adolescence. It was only when I reached full maturity that I was able to achieve true mastery over the strange abilities with which I had been entrusted. For the remainder of my life on earth, I was destined to occupy a permanent stance on the front line of a spiritual battle and was exposed to a constant battery of fire from both visible and invisible sources.

One may question why it is that some individuals develop gifts of psychic sensitivity while others seem immune to this whole mode of experience. Why is it that psychically sensitive individuals are permitted exclusive access to domains that are essentially invisible to the majority? The answer to this question is that such people possess a particularly astute spiritual 'receiving' mechanism. But it is also true to say that development of psychic sensitivity is ultimately within the reach of every human being upon the earth. However, in the majority of cases, such abilities lie dormant, undeveloped and unused. This is commensurate with the spiritual climate of the modern world, where the inner life has a tendency to be suppressed in deference to the more popular collective sport of materialism and ego-stroking. If humankind as a whole were to turn its attention inward instead of outward, psychic perceptiveness would begin to manifest itself in a much wider proportion of the earth's population. However, most people persist in allowing themselves to be distracted by covetousness and a hankering after outward position and status, which results in a situation where the inner life receives very short shrift indeed.

Regarding the essential purpose of psychic gifts, most Christian believers are conversant with the various Biblical warnings concerning their misuse. These cautions relate to the danger of reliance on powers and influences that have the potential to usurp the sovereignty and centrality of God within the heart. For the psychically sensitive believer, the only safe spiritual path is one where God perpetually reigns on the throne of the heart and where the state of psychic giftedness is constantly regulated and powered by the Divine.

Again, the human ego proves to be the main stumbling block here, in that it possesses the capability to entice towards the hypnotic lure of self-import and self-aggrandizement. In my own life, I came to realize that it is only when psychic gifts are wholeheartedly committed to God that they can be of any positive help to others. The selfish and egoistical use of psychic abilities always carries the underlying threat of contamination by dark forces. But in order for psychic gifts to be positively harnessed and correctly employed, the sensitive believer first needs to acquire a measure of enlightenment regarding their day to day handling.

During my priestly ministry of spiritual direction and counseling, many people sought my help in understanding and managing gifts of sensitivity. The first piece of advice I invariably gave was that such abilities should be completely abandoned to Almighty God. It is an unfortunate fact that the world of psychic sensitivity tends to be awash with individuals who insist on managing their abilities from the hub of their own inflated egos. Such people are, in some cases, well intentioned and in others frankly charlatan, but in both instances there remains the ever present danger of infiltration by dark powers. It cannot be stressed enough that, for the Christian believer, it is only when one is utterly rooted and grounded in the True Vine that gifts of sensitivity can remain pure, safely managed and properly employed. It is salutary to remember that Our Lord Himself, following His baptism, was not immune to temptation where His own spiritual abilities were concerned. We are given a vivid account of a severe time of testing in the wilderness, during which Christ was exposed to temptation after temptation, as the powers of darkness attempted to lure Him in the direction of personal glory.[2] Such experiences are all too common in the life of the sensitive believer and will occur again and again in all manner of different guises. The complete entrustment of psychic gifts to Almighty God once and for all places their use and management into the safest of hands. Subsequently, one will discover that these same gifts are given back in trust, but with a subtle difference. They will thereafter be Christified, empowered and undergirded by a Savior who will remain constantly alongside to guide in their correct use. This state of inner abandonment needs to be reinforced on a daily basis. Having relinquished one's gifts and abilities to Christ, the next step of importance is commitment to an ongoing daily habit of contemplative prayer. This should ideally be conducted within a relationship of sound and reliable spiritual direction. Having said this however, one should also remember that placing oneself in the hands of the wrong director is ultimately worse than having no guidance at all. In a situation where no obvious mentor appears on the horizon, one must pray each day for the inspiration of the Holy Spirit in the management of one's inner life. The only reliable source of guidance within the perplexing world of psychic sensitivity is Jesus Christ through the inspiration of the Holy Spirit. The overall aim is a state in which one is able to draw constantly from the indwelling power of Christ within the heart. It will thus become possible to befriend one's spiritual gifts and to place oneself in a position of positivity by using them to build up the body of Christ.

From the outset, the psychically sensitive Christian may experience a sense of inner claustrophobia at being called to live a life that appears to be perpetually invaded by the negative material of others. Indeed, it may sometimes prove difficult to manage one's own life successfully, while at the same time having to field an unremitting flow of diverse emotional traffic. Added to this, the sensitive believer may also be prey to attack from the various undesirable dark forces that exist within the collective consciousness. There is a New Testament passage which vividly describes the nature of the ongoing spiritual battle that is commonly faced by all Christians and which gives sound advice on spiritual self-protection. It uses the analogy of the battledress of a Roman soldier - a familiar sight in Biblical times.[3] The wise words remind the believer of the supremacy of Almighty God and that as Christians, we have access at all times to His unfailing help and protection. The passage goes on to describe the nature of our common spiritual enemy and gives reference to the constantly raging battle between darkness and light on the earth. The Eastern religions also offer helpful guidance in relation to the psychic centers that are situated within the auric field of the physical body. These centers are known as Chakra points and may be defined as portals of energy through which the sensitive individual may be vulnerable to attack from negative material. The Chakras are commonly thought to be situated at the base of the spine, the sacrum, the lumbar area, the heart, the base of the neck, the forehead and the crown of the head. Knowledge of the presence and position of these psychic doorways can be of immense help in learning to protect oneself from external spiritual threats. In relation to this, there is a simple meditative exercise which I found extremely useful during my lifetime on the earth. It involves entering a state of contemplative prayer and creating an inner mental picture of the Cross of Christ. One then needs to concentrate on breathing in and out in a controlled manner, while at the same time imagining that the passage of the breath is passing through the center of the Cross. This whole image is then placed imaginatively over the lowest Chakra point. The exercise should be practiced on a daily basis and one should progressively move up through each Chakra in turn, until one eventually reaches the crown of the head. In my own case this proved to be a useful and powerful method of internal imagery, which, once mastered, provided effective self-protection in situations when I was on the receiving end of undesirable psychic assault. It may perhaps sound like a lot of confused mumbo-jumbo to those who have never had occasion to experience psychic attack in any shape or form. But to those for whom such occurrences form the very mettle of daily existence, it will make perfect sense and may well prove to be a method worth trying.

The day to day experience of the psychically sensitive Christian thus consists of an ongoing and unremitting perception of the emotional and spiritual material of others, both individually and collectively. Such material is perceived in exactly the same way as one experiences one's own feelings and emotions, except that it eventually becomes possible to determine immediately when the origin is a source other than oneself. In other words, one's essential powers of discernment are perfected over time. When in congenial company alongside mutually supportive friends and contemporaries, one is able to perceive the presence of upbuilding and edifying material in the form of blessings of friendship and love. As one progresses through life, it eventually becomes possible to hone one's gifts, so that one is able to discern immediately and accurately the source of received feelings and emotions, especially when they originate from those one knows well. Incidentally, perception of this sort can also occur at a distance, even from many miles away. One also discovers that all psychic emanations bear the unique spiritual 'fingerprint' of the person concerned. But there will be countless instances where it is not immediately possible to identify the source of such emanations and in such cases, one should pray to the Holy Spirit for discernment as to how one should proceed. It needs to be underlined that the perception of material from other people is given solely for the purpose of intercessory prayer. Such abilities are categorically not given in order to be able to display one's psychic prowess or to bring attention to oneself or one's gifts. It goes without saying that material perceived from others should always be held in confidence and that one should resist the self-serving temptation to reveal one's knowledge to the person concerned or indeed to anyone else, unless one is specifically inspired to do so within the context of one's prayer. From the start, one should resolve to follow a strict personal code of confidentiality, prudence and honor when handling the delicate material of other people, commensurate with that of any counselor or doctor. Incidentally the ability to perceive the feelings and emotions of others is immensely helpful if one happens to be engaged in one of the helping professions. For example, in a counseling situation, one has the innate ability to detect undercurrents of distress or negativity of which the person themselves may either be consciously unaware or unable to express. This may lead to important clues and insights relating to the nature of the underlying problem, which then may go on to assist the practitioner towards appropriate ministry and treatment. The same will be true in any situation where one is in the position of trying to help others - either in a professional sense or simply in the course of one's everyday existence. As one progresses along the journey of the inner life and as one becomes grounded and centered in the light of God's love, the aim is to become adept in blessing others with a positive anointing of love and healing. It is thus possible to flow out in a constructive and helpful way towards one's neighbor from the lighted center of one's prayer. One will then become a positive instrument of healing to the glory of Almighty God. A spiritual state of this sort is attained after much time and much scrupulous inner work, the ultimate aim being that one becomes a spotlessly clear channel that is uncontaminated by one's own material both past and present.

The underside of psychic giftedness is that one is also often prey to assault from the negative emanations of others and on some occasions, one may possibly find oneself in social situations of embarrassing disparity. For instance, one may be engaged in supposed pleasantries with another individual, while at the same time one is on the receiving end of dark emissions of jealousy, dislike or other such negativity. The person in question will, of course, be under the complacent assumption that their true feelings are being successfully concealed within the bounds of their own mind and heart. In cases of such inconsistency, it is well-nigh impossible to continue along the lines of pleasant conversation and to maintain any degree of outward calm, while at the same time being aware of such waves of ill-intent. However, as one progresses further into the light of God, negativity on the part of others becomes increasingly irrelevant. It is important to remember that each of us is on a progressive inner journey and that negative emotions are invariably a symptom of inner woundedness or perceived personal inadequacy. The said person may also be completely unaware of the trigger of their own negativity, which quite often relates to painful events in their early life. One should therefore do one's best to turn the proverbial cheek in exactly the same way as one would aim to do as a Christian when outwardly challenged by negative behavior. The ideal is that such occasions should be regarded as an opportunity to flow out in love and healing towards the individual concerned. One should also remember that all judgement of others is ultimately the domain of God and that negative emissions, whether displayed outwardly or concealed, are His business not ours. Meditating on appropriate and supportive words of Scripture within one's heart can be very helpful in steering a positive course in such instances.

15.

PSYCHIC SENSITIVITY (2)

An area that travels hand in hand with psychic sensitivity is that of communication by telepathy. This is an ability that will become second nature once one reaches the greater life of eternity. But for some acutely sensitive individuals it is a mode of communication that proves possible while on the earth. Such conversations are not only expressed in words but also include the transmission of the entirety of oneself, no holds barred. Whole chunks of life experience are thus able to be conveyed and received. Full knowledge of the other comes in a flash and one is immediately able to perceive all of their previous experiences, as if they were one's own, from the time of their birth and sometimes even before that. One always has control however over how much one 'lets in' at any given time. The inner equipment that permits such an exchange is present within the mind of every human being on earth, but in most cases this ability has been lost due to the present day propensity towards elective spiritual blindness. Communication by telepathy is initiated by concentrating thought waves in the direction of the person with whom one wishes to communicate - someone known to be in possession of a comparable gift. It will then become possible to conduct a conversation by expressing and receiving thoughts, emotions and concepts within the bounds of the mind. The process takes some practice and can initially prove somewhat mentally exhausting, as one is using cerebral 'muscles' that may have been little exercised in the past. Such communication cannot happen at all unless both parties consent to the conversation and it is never possible for the mind to be invaded in any sense. As one might imagine, it would be a perfect nuisance if all manner of material was able to be projected into one's thoughts willy-nilly. The concept of stalking would take on a whole new meaning in such a case. I must also underline here that within each person's heart there exists a sacred and private area into which no one but God has access. This hidden 'cave' is the place where the soul is able to commune in absolute privacy with its Maker. Telepathic communication cannot ever invade this sacred area and is a mode of conversation which takes place entirely within the mind. As such it is conducted on the very periphery of the human consciousness. The execution of the telepathic process could perhaps be likened to a game of inner 'tennis', in that thoughts and concepts are able to be steadily 'volleyed' back and forth. As such, the initiating individual begins by lobbing a stream of communicatory material into the psychic field of the recipient, who then decides whether or not they find it convenient or prudent to continue with the conversation at that time. As in the case of discourse on the telephone, either person may choose to put down the 'receiver' at any time and there always has to be mutual consent for the conversation to proceed. Once such a communicatory relationship has become properly established, it becomes progressively easier for conversation to take place between two individuals. Frequency of communication will eventually result in the carving out of a familiar and well-used two-way pathway. A relationship of trust is also gradually developed as one shares one's essential nature, defining faults, foibles, past history and present experience. Thus, within the bounds of such a relationship, each becomes increasingly comfortable, relaxed and free in the presence of the other. As mentioned earlier, this form of communication will prove second nature in the life of eternity and is something that happens quite naturally over here. Once one reaches the greater life, one will find it possible to share the essence of one's being with all who exist on a comparable spiritual wavelength. However, those on a lower spiritual frequency are never permitted communicatory access to souls on a greater spiritual wavelength. The essential rule, both on the earthly level and in the life beyond death, is that one must be resonant in kind with those with whom one shares in this way. Souls of a higher resonance have the ability to 'scan' souls on a lower spiritual wavelength, which proves extremely useful in the work of healing on this side of being. Telepathic communication, as this piece of collaborative writing proves, is also possible between this world and the next.

Another element of psychic sensitivity involves the discernment of emanations from the unseen world. Before addressing this subject, it is necessary to refer to the various warnings and exhortations within Scripture relating to this area. If one studies these properly, one will notice that these admonitions focus on the concept of 'calling up' spiritual entities in the mediumistic sense. The practice of such ill-advised dabbling carries the risk of placing oneself in extreme spiritual danger. The important delineation between the perception of such communication in the Christian sense and that of mediumistic contact can be focused on the words 'call up'. The latter is something which a Christian should never ever attempt under any circumstances. As mentioned elsewhere, Christian psychic sensitivity should be perpetually undergirded by a strong and steady inner life of contemplative prayer and one's sole focus should remain on Almighty God at all times. But if one happens to possess a gift of psychic sensitivity, contemplative prayer may also yield the added ability to be able to perceive discarnate presences. If one begins to experience such phenomena, it is necessary immediately to call upon Almighty God for protection and spiritual guidance. When I found myself receiving such perceptions during my Christian ministry, I would begin a repetition of the Name of Jesus in the form of the Jesus

Prayer[1] and would intersperse this with recitations of the Our Father. The expounding of the Name of Christ carries with it such overriding power that one is immediately granted complete spiritual protection. In a similar way, recitation of the Lord's Prayer provides a type of mystical cloak which serves to anoint the surrounding atmosphere with the light of God's power and love. Therefore, the important demarcation line that separates mediumship from psychic sensitivity in the Christian sense can be found in the basic difference between the words 'call up' and 'perceive'. To underline the essential point once again, the Christian sensitive should never attempt, of their own volition, to 'call up' or to 'make contact' with discarnate spirits. In the life of the sensitive believer, such spiritual perceptions may occur as a sideline of contemplative prayer - prayer which is entirely focused on God alone. The dangers of mediumistic independent attempts to contact discarnate souls are manifold. In so doing, one risks uncovering a Pandora's box of potential problems and spiritual threats. There are dangerous malign forces in existence which are capable of causing all manner of mischief. But if, in the context of Christ-centered prayer, one finds oneself in possession of a gift of perceiving discarnate souls, it may be concluded that such contact has been permitted by God for intercessory purposes. For within the spiritual realms there are souls who are unable to move forward into the light of God's love. The reason for this is various. In some cases, such souls may not possess any concept of spiritual belief and may be weighed down by negative feelings of guilt, fear and unworthiness. There may also be the presence of unfinished agendas or issues. For instance, the soul may feel that he or she is in possession of a piece of information which needs to be urgently imparted to someone on the earth before they are able to move on. Perhaps a crime of violence has been the cause of death and there is a resulting desire to see justice done. Alternatively there may be a strong emotional attachment to another person, whom the soul finds it difficult to leave behind.

Assisting trapped souls towards liberation and peace formed a regular and essential part of my priestly ministry on earth. The task at hand is to enlighten the communicating soul to the redemptive healing power of Jesus Christ and then to pray the soul onward into the light of God's love. It was always a great moment when I witnessed the release of such souls into the light and was able to observe their eventual progression towards the greater life of eternity. It is important to note that this type of intercession is immensely powerful when implemented from the earth plane. This is why earthbound prayers for the dead are so terribly important. In this way, trapped souls may be liberated into the light of God's everlasting love. The most effective spiritual tool in this area is, of course, the Requiem Mass. But there are also those on the earth who possess specific spiritual gifts in the area of 'boatman' work, of which I myself was formerly an example. There is much work to be done in this domain, as there are countless souls who are desperately in need of healing and liberation. Such work is not plain sailing in every case, as some souls persist in finding it difficult to let go of things earthly and to move forward into the light of God. In such cases, severe problems occur during the process of transition to the greater life. Most people are familiar with the concept of 'ghosts' and eerie tales of 'things going bump in the night' and that sort of thing. Much hype on this subject habitually appears within the medium of film, television and popular novels. There is generally a lot of fear connected to this area and it remains an essentially shadowy and elusive subject to our ken while we are on the earth. But the true meaning of the word 'ghost' is simply that portion of an individual which exists apart from the body - the discarnate element as it were. Ghosts are souls who, for one reason or another, are unable to move forward into the light of God. They are essentially trapped on the lower level of psychic consciousness which is on a parallel to the earth plane. In some cases, souls have completely repelled the fact of bodily death and have blocked out all knowledge that this has occurred. In such instances a soul may succeed in building a protective psychic 'box' which then becomes lodged in a loop of time. In an attempt to successfully block out the fact of physical death, the soul may then try to perpetuate an illusion of ongoing earthly life by the incessant carrying out of a familiar task or agenda. They are often visible to the psychically sensitive and commonly appear dressed in the manner of the era in which they formerly existed. Until such time as they consent to accept the fact of their passage from the earth to the greater life, they are not able to move forward at all. This is an extremely sad state of affairs and one which requires ongoing and dedicated intercessory prayer on the part of the psychically astute on the earth. C. S. Lewis, in his children's book; 'The Last Battle' gives a vivid and illuminative analogy of a comparable fictional situation. He relates the story of a group of souls who have recently passed over to the greater life, but who are then unable to see the wonder, beauty and invitation of eternity that is beckoning them forward. They persist in adhering to a collective belief that they are trapped in a place of darkness - a scenario that is entirely of their own making. Their plight is described thus: 'Their prison is only in their own minds, yet they are in that prison; and so afraid of being taken in that they cannot be taken out.'[2] But the irresistible draw of the light and love of God will eventually serve to bring about release. Souls will thus be enabled to detach themselves from the earth and will be able encompass the immutable fact that the larger picture of eternity is calling them onward.

In my own case, experiences of the perception of discarnate souls first occurred during my early teens. This was initially very disquieting to say the least, mainly due to my belief at first that I had no control over such happenings. I read widely and voraciously on the subject in an attempt to learn more, but I subsequently discovered that most books on the subject were invariably sensationalistic or just plain 'weird'. My parents, as one can perhaps imagine from what I have already shared elsewhere about my dysfunctional family, were obviously going to be of no help whatsoever. It was immediately clear that this whole area was completely beyond the bounds of their life experience. Thankfully, the aforementioned David proved to be an immense source of help in taking away my fear and passing on his own extensive well of knowledge. My experience of perceiving discarnate souls always happened in exactly the same way. In an attempt to accurately convey the process of such perception, it is perhaps useful to imagine the scenario of being completely alone in a room. Then stretch the imagination a little further to include the concept of another person silently entering the room and assuming a hidden position out of the line of one's peripheral vision. Even those who do not consider themselves to be 'psychic' in any shape or form will normally be able to 'sense' the presence of another person before they see them visually. Most people therefore have the ability to perceive accurately when they 'have company', so to speak, within the bounds of any limited physical space. In the case of psychic perception, the sensitive person knows immediately when they are in the presence of a discarnate soul, but of course has no way of proving this to anyone else. The initial process of discerning the presence of a discarnate entity invariably begins with the perception of the emotional state of the soul in question, in that the auric periphery of the soul contains essential emotional characteristics. The sensitive person may also be granted a physical glimpse of the soul in the form of an inner or outer picture. But in reality, all such 'seeing' occurs at soul level using the deepest part of the spiritual consciousness. Once such a perception has occurred, it is necessary immediately to call upon the Name of Jesus Christ for guidance about how one should proceed and to afford spiritual protection. If the manifestation is malign, the Name of Christ will serve to disperse it immediately. But if it is genuine in form and intent and proves to be a soul in need of help, the utterance of the Name of Christ will serve to bring divine light and power into the exchange. I was in my early teens when such an experience first occurred in my own life - an incident that will be etched on my consciousness for evermore. One night, while awaiting sleep, I became spiritually aware of a sort of 'cloud' of oppressive sadness all around me. This was followed by the projection of a visual image into my mind - the figure of an African slave. He was unkempt, scantily dressed and his body was covered in weals and sores. The expression on his face was one of pure, unmitigated sorrow. I then received the overwhelming conviction that I was required to help in some way and there followed a two-way telepathic exchange - a process that immediately felt as natural to me as if it had occurred a thousand times before. At the same time, I began to receive a flow of interior spiritual guidance as to how I should proceed. I first asked the name of the soul, whereupon the word 'Thomas' was impressed upon my mind. Then I asked: 'Am I able to help you in any way?' This brought forth a rapid flow of information conveyed in words and pictures. It transpired that Thomas had been a servant in the house many years previously. Graphic scenes of violent beatings began to tumble into my mind one after the other. On the sidelines I saw a woman heavy with child whom I perceived to be Thomas's wife. It became clear that the punishments had been precipitated by the displacement of a sum of money, which Thomas had been wrongly accused of stealing. The brutality of the assaults I was shown seemed to stretch on interminably, eventually resulting in Thomas's death. Then a similar punishment was meted out upon the woman, serving to bring about the miscarriage of her baby. I perceived that since his passing Thomas had remained in a state of profound anger and unrest. I then felt moved to ask Thomas if he could see a light anywhere in his vicinity. He affirmed that, since his passing, he had always been able to see a light in the distance, but that now it was becoming clearer to him. I myself then caught a glimpse of the blaze of transcendent glory that he described - a wondrous vision exuding an intense sense of love, joy and peace. Enfolded in its center I saw the figure of Thomas's wife and in her arms she held a baby. When he saw his wife, Thomas's face broke into a glorious smile. At once he moved into the center of the light and disappeared from view. The inner vision abruptly faded and once again I found myself alone. But the memory of the encounter stayed with me and served to inspire me forever more. Thomas was my first 'client' as it were in the area of boatman work - there were to be countless others over the years. In each instance the soul would possess an inability to progress towards the light of God's love, due to overwhelming negative emotions such as anger, fear or guilt. My own role was that of a spiritual catalyst of healing. It was intensely satisfying work, but at the same time it proved somewhat lonely as I was rarely able to share it with other people. I was always afraid to mention such occurrences in the company of my Christian friends in case I was met by cries of 'heresy' and I did not wish to mar the beautiful experiences by inviting any sort of a negative response. I was eventually to find freedom of expression among a group of like-minded friends with whom I found I shared a common spiritual experience. This helped enormously, as it served to quench the innate sense of 'homelessness' that one invariably experiences as a sensitive within the Christian Church. Thus I was able to find a congenial social circle where I was fortunate enough to be able to form deep and lasting friendships with others who experienced life on a similar spiritual wavelength.

 Those who are psychically sensitive often also possess an ability to perceive auric emanations around human forms, sacred objects, buildings or places. Such perceptions may either be outwardly visible or spiritually discerned. The human aura commonly concentrates itself around the head area and as such, color and form can be immensely beautiful. Each individual aura is unique and reflects the spiritual blueprint of the soul concerned. In the advanced soul, an aura is capable of spreading over a very large distance and casts a benevolent blessing on all in its path. Auric emanations prove extremely useful in the context of the earthly healing ministry and serve to draw the attention of the practitioner to hidden problems in need of attention. Conversely, auric presences around buildings or geographical places are more commonly perceived, while they remain largely invisible to the naked eye. In the latter case, many people, whether they consider themselves to be psychically attuned or not, have the ability to discern 'atmospheres' of positivity or negativity. Parish clergy will sometimes receive requests to administer a blessing when a persistent sense of malignancy has been perceived within a particular building. The result will be the introduction of positive spiritual vibrations resulting in a 'domino' effect of positivity spreading within the material structure. Similarly, in the case of a new Church building or a house of prayer, a priestly blessing will serve to ensure a good beginning in that place.

In the life of eternity, personal auric emanations are more commonly perceived. In the context of a group soul such as AVESHIDA, each member possesses and displays an individual aura and the group also shares an aura in common. On the earth, in the context of a cohesive group sharing a common aim such as a monastic community, such auric communion is built up over time. The resulting spiritual harmony is capable of instilling positive vibrations within the collective consciousness and serves to bring healing to the world at large.

In the general sense, those who try to 'demonize' psychic sensitivity within the Christian life miss out on so much. Blocking this whole area of experiential richness serves to limit and contain the power of Christ into a narrow way of thinking, which has the effective of cauterizing spiritual growth. It results in a blinkered attitude that favors the concept of a 'safe' spirituality overseen by a biddable, Father-Christmas-like God. But those Christian sensitives who find themselves frustrated by such apparent spiritual blindness, would do well to remember a point previously mentioned:

that each soul journeys towards God with as much light and truth as it can bear. It is therefore necessary to strive to flow out in compassion and love towards those believers who are presently only able to accept a more diluted version of Christ's infinite power and glory. But it doesn't take much imagination to construe the potential usefulness of gifts of psychic sensitivity for good within the worldwide Church. Such gifts are endowed by the power of love and are given in order to assist, enhance and edify the Christian experience. Psychic sensitivity is aligned to mysticism, an area that has been present in all its varied forms in the Church since earliest times. Psychic experience is therefore nothing new, and if Christ is at our center He will protect us from all ill-advised paths and tangents. Truth is what we are all essentially seeking and the recognition and acceptance of God's abundant gifts to all.

16.

LIGHTING THE PATH

From the very moment of their creation, angels are entirely given to God and are wholly at one with the Divine. As such they are an extension of the glory of God. As an allegory, one could perhaps compare them to an army of marching ants, in that they have a similar collaborative and integrative way of achieving any aim. The company of angels possesses perfect unity and oneness of being. The greatest of all are the illustrious and powerful archangels - the fighting angels of combat who wear protective armor and wield mighty swords. Michael, the leader, is tall, proud, battle-scarred and golden. His wings echo with a myriad of rainbow lights and he carries a glittering sword. He stands within an aura of gold and his battle cry reverberates throughout the spheres. Blessed Gabriel appears within an eddy of purple lights and his face is surrounded by a blurring lace of fluttering wings. Jegudiel is shrouded in green whirlpools of light and his face is indeed conventionally 'angelic' - soft and beautiful. Raphael, the blessed angel of healing, has large diaphanous blue wings and his eyes tell a million tales of gentle ministry. Uriel, the angel of fire, is surrounded by flame and has a single, startling magnesium strobe of white light within the chest area. It is necessary to shield one's eyes when in his blessed presence. Selaphiel has plumes of peacock-like feathers and is imbued with all manner of exquisite colors. In appearance, angels are very beautiful, and their color and form can be breathtaking to behold. But in the capacity of the work of guardianship, they look very much like you or I. In other words, their appearance is entirely functional and appropriate for the work at hand. Occasionally, they will permit themselves to be sighted, if this deems to be advantageous in terms of encouragement. They also have the ability to change form simply by the power of thought, and as such are able to adopt whatever mode of being is needful at any given moment in time. Most people have heard of wondrous stories of angelic intervention and it is true that an angel will step in, in the event that their charge meets with any danger at all. Situations, in other words, that may result in harm which will cut short earthly life before the appointed time. Angels are also capable of swift travel, but this does not always necessarily warrant a pair of wings. Incidentally, all of us, on this side of being, are able to move from place to place relatively easily. It is all a case of willing such an action to be so by the use of one's thoughts. I, in actual fact, was able to travel in this way, in the spiritual sense, during my lifetime on the earth. Without wishing to boast at all, I was extremely well versed in this skill by the time I reached the heavenly realms.

The throne of God is surrounded with an angelic hierarchy of praise - a sight that is unbelievably beautiful to behold. When I first saw it, it felt that the bottom had dropped out of my world, in the sense that all of my prior conceptions proved to be completely inaccurate in every way possible. Whatever you think now and whatever you imagine, multiply it several thousand times and you may perhaps be close, but you will still be a long way off. Imagine the concept of the aurora borealis - the display of lights that at times is visible on the earth. Imagine the glorious colors of rainbows and the wonder of the beauty of the stars. I struggle to describe it all in earthly terms and I am really quite unable to convey it to you at all. I also find it impossible to describe the sound of the millions of voices raised in song and the festal shout that has the effect of sweeping one right up within it, until one is veritably flying and soaring in the middle of a melody of sound.

Part of the work of the group AVESHIDA is to assist these emissaries of light by descending periodically to the realms of darkness to rescue lost souls. Those who have found themselves in this terrible place by accident or mistake. There are gradients of darkness within these lower spheres and radiating outwards are ever lessening areas of darkness. Within the perimeter of the gloom are souls who, while on the earth, made a series of errors and mistakes, through their own weakness or woundedness. They do not ultimately want to be in this darkness and in their hearts, albeit dimly, the divine light of love, goodness and truth continues to shine. The imprint of the Divine exists within their deepest heart. These are the ones who belong to the Father.

During such work of rescue and healing, we travel in groups in order to sustain each other in the spiritual sense. We initially hold a meeting on the Seventh Level and one of our number - Cloud normally, or sometimes Mabel - will go to the plane of childhood where Marylu dwells. They then accompany her back for the purpose of our meeting. Once we are all assembled, we sit in a circle for our preliminary session of prayer. In the center, a light appears which is the collective consciousness of the entire group. And then we discuss - ideas flowing back and forth from our minds and hearts through the light of the collective consciousness and back to each other. In this way, everybody shares fully what they are thinking and feeling individually. There is no judgement of the opinions of the others and no disagreement at all. Our individual thoughts and feelings are simply absorbed and assimilated by everybody until we are of one mind. An angelic presence then manifests within the circle and his mind (I say 'his' for ease, as angels are not of one particular gender, except in the case of the Archangels, who are male simply because physical strength is an advantage in their case). The angel's mind absorbs our discussion and he/she (shall I say 'he' - I hope that those of you who mind about these things will not mind - male and female are equally celebrated here in any case). And he - the angel - accompanies us to the place of our work. When we depart, we always inform one of the higher echelons of light beforehand, so that they can pray for us and hold us in the light of God while we are away.

While carrying out a work of rescue, we descend to these outer reaches of darkness. We find ourselves a place in which to operate and then we stand in a circle and begin our prayer. In so doing we muster up as much light and love as we are able. If one imagines the searchlight of a boat in a dense fog - our light similarly competes with the gloom and the blackness. Then we begin to repeat in unison, that most precious of all names - the blessed Name of Jesus Christ. The utterance of His Name acts like a blaze of light that breaks through the intensity of the swirling darkness and shines a spotlight upon the hiding places of lost souls.

To give an example of such work, our group was recently asked by intercessors on the earth plane to look into the case of a tragic suicide. I will refer to the soul concerned as 'John' in order to protect his identity. On the subject of suicide, it is necessary to draw out the reasoning behind the act of violence, for most such triggers originate from wounds in childhood or even before that. The emotional charge behind such an act has to be very powerful, for it essentially goes against all of man's natural survival instincts to deliberately draw a close to one's life. This is an act of violence that is very serious indeed.

On the occasion in question, we descended as a group to a place of very great darkness. How do we know where to go? Well, the power of a name comes into play here. We homed in on the name we had been given. On this particular occasion, we descended to a place of very great gloom. There was no light there at all, just a type of swirling blackness. Not only in the visual sense, but an emotional and spiritual darkness also. We sustain each other within the group during this type of work, by the light within our minds and hearts. We maintain a link of light with each other throughout. If one of us is overcome or distressed by what we see or what we encounter, the others then draw closely around to hold them in the collective light of the group until recovery has been assured. On this occasion, as we homed in on the soul in question, we were swept into his gloom. Emanating from John, in bands of intense darkness, was the sheer psychic terror of what he had experienced.

I will divert for a moment to speak of suicide and what it means in the life hereafter. Suicide is a state of being - a terrible sin in the eyes of humankind - to destroy one's life and to spit in the face of God as it were. But suicide is in fact a symptom of the state of mind and soul of a devastated individual who is so overcome by sorrow and pain that to draw another breath becomes unthinkable and impossible. It is commonly to do with woundedness, of the mind and heart and usually relates to an event or series of events in the person's deepest past. If one looks around at present society - at those who derive comfort from pacifiers such as drugs, alcohol and sex - this is almost always to do with unbearable inner woundedness. Sometimes an event or series of events is so deeply buried that the person concerned is not consciously aware of where the trouble lies. The mind thus protects the heart from material that cannot be borne. I myself was such a wounded person having suffered abuse at the hands of my father. But I was fortunate in that God in His Grace provided me with people who appeared at just the right time to help me to defuse this unexploded bomb of anger within my heart. Others are not so fortunate. This is where psychotherapy and counseling can prove to be so useful, in that this provides a safe environment where a person may explore past pain and may come to terms with it in a supportive atmosphere of love. It allows them to relive painful occurrences and to release their negative emotional charge. One may consider those in society who rely on substances and promiscuity and are unable to maintain any sort of normal lifestyle at all. This is invariably a symptom of a 'soul sickness' so deep and has its root at some point in the person's past.

But to continue with John's story. We, as a group, homed in on his name and we eventually came across him in an area of abject darkness. We stood in a circle nearby and prayed for some time, linking up spiritually with the higher echelons of light on the Seventh Level. All we could hear to begin with was John's pitiful crying and his calling out repeatedly the name of one who had been very dear to him. Eventually, when we had summoned enough light for our work to proceed, one of our number (in this case Cloud) walked away from our circle and entered into John's darkness while the rest of us continued nearby in prayer. As Cloud approached, the light of his presence gave rise to the creation of a tree, which sprouted forth a short distance from where John sat. The tree then grew rapidly until it had reached full height. John stood up, walked over and sat down beside it. Then Cloud's creativity came into play once again. A short distance from the tree he caused a small fire to come into being. Cloud sat cross-legged beside the fire and began to gaze into its flames. John stood up again and then sat down beside the fire. Cloud took a lighted stick and began to draw in the dust beside the fire. He drew the sign of the Cross. Then, within the flames, there appeared an image of John's death by suicide. This was then replaced by an image of the loved ones upon whom great distress and pain had been inflicted by his untimely death. Further images served to confirm that John's suicide had been triggered by woundedness in his deepest past, of which he had never been consciously aware. The end of the story is that we were able to begin to bring about healing for John and set him on the path towards light and truth. The suffering of John's past which had been the root cause of his situation was eventually able to be addressed. We continue to follow his journey. We will never let him go in any sense.

On the earth also, once one reaches a certain level of spiritual maturity, the opportunity may present itself to help and guide one's fellow souls. In such work it is necessary to be able to 'tune in' at heart level with those one is called to assist. Passive prayerful listening on many different levels is required, alongside firm guidance and a prevailing attitude of deep compassion. One needs the sensitivity to gently uncover innate strengths and abilities; while at the same time calmly recognizing foibles and weaknesses, in a spirit of charity and love. The guidance of souls is never ever about authoritarianism or blindly giving orders, but about enabling one's charges to be as excellent as they can possibly be. The role also requires emotional maturity, in that one must be prepared eventually to allow those in one's care to discover the potential of directing themselves, often without their consciously realizing that they are beginning to do so. In other words, one needs to be able to forgo all need to 'shine' in one's own right and be able to lead from behind with encouragement and kindness.

The role of spiritual leadership, at its most effective, is all about dying to oneself in order to allow others to blossom. We may look to Our Lord as the prime example here. When He eventually took leave of His disciples at the time of His Ascension, He left them as men and women transformed - a previously motley crew that had faithfully supported and traveled alongside Him during the course of His earthly mission. These were individuals who had tentatively and tremulously begun the journey and had eventually succeeded in becoming something more, simply by virtue of the journey itself. From the very start, the disciples were presented in the Gospels as a collection of rough-necked, thoroughly worldly individuals. Through Christ's nurturing presence and subtle influence, they were gradually gifted with the dignity and truth of their own beings and were enabled to become what they were created to be - whole, complete and sound.

Spiritual leadership often involves complete forgetfulness of self and a surrender of one's own hopes and dreams, in order that one's charges might take the final bow. In the dying Savior on the Cross, we are able to behold the perfect example of self-sublimating leadership in action. The essentials of Christian leadership may be contained in one word - 'sacrifice' - in that the role is not about becoming a star in one's own right or about attaining some sort of celebrity status, but rather about disappearing so that others may eventually take the final glory.

God does seem to have a habit of choosing extremely unlikely candidates for the role of spiritual leadership. As St Paul declares in his letter to the Church in Corinth: 'To shame the wise, God has chosen what the world counts folly, and to shame what is strong, God has chosen what the world counts weakness. He has chosen things without rank or standing in the world, mere nothings, to overthrow the existing order.'[1] Indeed, many of the great spiritual leaders of Old Testament times initially baulked at and denied their calling. One such case was Jeremiah - an individual who had been earmarked by God for the task of preparing receptive souls for divinely inspired events that were to come. From the very start, he violently protested his unsuitability crying: 'Ah! Lord God, - - I am not skilled in speaking; I am too young.'[2] Almighty God then proceeded to admonish him for his reticence and lack of confidence: 'Do not plead that you are too young; for you are to go to whatever people I send you, and say whatever I tell you to say.'[3] Similarly, when an apparently poorly equipped shepherd boy was selected by God as the successor to the crown of Israel, His decision was qualified by the words: 'The Lord does not see as a mortal sees; mortals see only appearances but the Lord sees into the heart.'[4] The prophet Isaiah later received a powerful revelation about the coming Messiah: 'I the Lord have called you with righteous purpose and taken you by the hand; I have formed you, and destined you to be a light for peoples, a lamp for nations, to open eyes that are blind, to bring captives out of prison, out of the dungeon where they lie in darkness.'[5] Words that are later quoted by Our Lord at the start of His earthly ministry.

In the context of today's fractured and ailing world, the role of spiritual leadership will often be accompanied by its sister ministry of healing. It is a sad fact of modern times that many people carry inner trauma and hurt of one sort or another, especially relating to the vulnerable period of childhood. Many individuals arrive at the cusp of adulthood in an emotionally wounded state. The spiritual guide may thus receive confidences, in the course of his or her ministry, of past scenarios of parental mental cruelty, or the deliberate withholding of love and affection. Incidentally, the latter can prove just as deeply wounding as physical abuse and has the propensity to cause arrested emotional growth. Such damage, when inflicted early on at the hands of a parent, has the effect of stunting the person's development and serves to prevent whole areas of the personality from functioning in an optimal way. The origins of such bad parenting may often be traced back to a recurring pattern of dysfunctional relationships within the infrastructure of the family unit and may be rooted in a tainted familial line. During my own earthly ministry, I periodically came across instances where whole family trees had been distorted and damaged, causing generation upon generation of unhappiness and deep pain. In such situations, the root cause of the dysfunction needed to be isolated, followed by healing prayer to effect a severance of bondage to the troubled area of malignancy within the family tree. Only then was full liberation achieved. In these cases it is necessary to detect whether the problem originates on the paternal or maternal side of lineage and it is helpful to hold a requiem for the last family member who has died on this side. This will have the positive effect of 'cauterizing' the line causing pain and distress to family members now living. But it is a very large and complicated subject and one which I cannot hope to adequately address within the scope of this book.[6]

Before one even considers entering the specialist area of Christian healing, it is vital to ascertain that one has received a directive from God to undertake such a role. The validity of such a call needs careful prayerful discernment, with the aid of one's spiritual guide, over a considerable period of time. If God is calling an individual to this path, He will make it abundantly clear and will direct the exact nature of the ministry. One simply cannot begin to interfere ill-advisedly in the lives of other people, until one has reached a significant level of wholeness within oneself. To even think of embarking on a ministry of the 'doctoring' of others, while one is in a state of inherent woundedness, is extremely dangerous indeed. For in so doing, one will repeatedly come up against one's own wounds and foibles, which may result in causing severe and lasting damage to those in one's charge. As Our Lord clearly advocates in the Gospels: 'It is not the healthy who need a doctor, but the sick,'[7] and again: 'Physician, heal yourself!'[8] During my own priestly ministry I was all too often called to the task of rescuing souls who were in virtual tatters after having received errant and ill-advised 'ministry' from other unhealed souls. One may perhaps question why anyone would even consider trying to minister to others when in fact it was they themselves who clearly need help. Regrettably, the answer once again may be found in the area of the ego. For in the vivid imaginations of such pseudo-healers exists an entirely fictional picture of themselves as being upon a pedestal of spiritual perfection. Such wounded individuals are often charismatic in nature - those, in other words, who possess considerable personal magnetism and 'drawing power'. They are generally people who enjoy the notion of their own supremacy and the attention and acclamation that their supposed 'healing gift' brings. They sometimes even manage to inveigle themselves into positions of authority, where they proceed to bolster up their already burgeoning egos by gaining control over vulnerable souls who are unfortunate enough to fall under their thrall. Ultimately, they have the potential to cause havoc in the lives of the already wounded, while all of the time remaining dangerously blinkered to their own glaring need for ministry. Sadly, their one aim is the maintenance of a self-gratifying, steady spotlight upon themselves. If you discern anger in my tone here, this is righteous indignation caused by the memory of encounters with spiritual quackery on far too many occasions during my earthly ministry. Sometimes I even had occasion to discover scenarios of whole groups who had blindly allowed themselves to be managed and manipulated by a deviant personality. I am not going to mention any names here - but suffice it to say - one should beware and one should keep one's eyes firmly and resolutely open. As Our Lord warns: 'Beware of false prophets, who come to you dressed up as sheep while underneath they are savage wolves.'[9] A ministry of healing is ideally carried out under the protecting umbrella of a parish or Christian community - situations where one will often come across people seeking support and guidance on their individual journeys towards wholeness. In very rare cases there are hallowed souls who have the strength, fortitude and spiritual advancement to embark on such a ministry without a comparable framework of support.

It is the duty of all spiritual guides to strive to live exemplary lives that are constantly saturated with prayer. One should seek to gird oneself with a steady drip feed of all that is good and positive, in order to maintain a spiritual state that is perpetually soaked in the light and love of Christ. As St Paul reminds us: 'All that is true, all that is noble, all that is just and pure, all that is lovable and attractive, whatever is excellent and admirable - fill your thoughts with these things.'[10] One should constantly beware of the illusory light - that which serves to ape the glory of Christ and aims to lead down thorny paths that are devoid of Christ's humble blessing of simple peace - and should try to live on a spiritual level at all times, fixing one's gaze unswervingly on Christ and

His eternal and glorious truth. It is very necessary to be ever on one's guard.

It is necessary to mention that spiritual leadership may sometimes involve encounters with the sobering area of malign phenomena. Opposition by the powers of darkness is part and parcel of the Christian life and no believer should ever ignore, gloss over or dilute the fact that such danger exists. I would often find myself approached for advice on this subject during my earthly ministry. While many in the Church showed discomfort in the face of my psychic abilities, it was a completely different story when those same individuals found themselves having to cope with the unknown quantity of spiritual malignancy within their own parishes. On such occasions, urgent pleas for assistance would proceed to hotfoot themselves to my door. In negotiating the foothills of the Christian journey, most people set out in a state of innate unhealedness and spiritual vulnerability. If any areas of weakness exist, be they spiritual, physical or psychological, the powers of darkness will make it their business to winkle them out and will not hesitate to try to shamelessly exacerbate them. The enemy is wily and will stop at nothing to unsettle and usurp a Christian soul, the general aim being to induce as much doubt, fear and confusion as possible. The acquirement of deep self-knowledge through individual inner work under the guidance of a spiritual mentor is an essential asset in remaining a step ahead of the enemy. Progress in the spiritual life leads to gradual healing of wounds past and present and such areas of vulnerability will thankfully grow fewer. But no one should ever assume themselves to have reached safe immunity from danger in the ongoing spiritual battle. The overriding and immutable fact to remember is that the power of Christ is greater than all things. On the earthly spiritual journey there are two forms of protection against which nothing is equal - the power of the Name of Jesus and the power of Christ's victory on the Cross. If one finds oneself under malign attack in any shape or form, the utterance of the Name of

Christ will bring immediate and complete protection. No Christian should ever be foolish enough to stand around in apparent helplessness when faced with the possibility of malign threat. An attitude of positive, commonsensical assertiveness is necessary just as much in the spiritual life as in the maelstrom of everyday existence in the modern world. Christ is of course ever present in the lives of all believers, but it is also needful to take responsibility for the safety of one's own soul by making use of the spiritual weapons that have been entrusted at the start of the journey. Whatever the nature of one's individual gift, every Christian has the ability to command malign forces to leave in Jesus' Name and to assert their working knowledge of the power of Christ's victory on the Cross. Dark powers are unpleasant and frightening, but once challenged by the Name of Christ they are immediately chained and can do no further harm.

Malicious attacks by the powers of darkness normally present themselves in one of two forms - directly or catalytically through the emotional woundedness of others. The latter does not imply that such individuals are intrinsically evil. Demonic possession is thankfully rare as is the complicity with rank evil that leads to such a state. The emotionally wounded, to a greater or lesser extent, simply possess inner areas of weakness which the powers of darkness may attempt to manipulate. If the said person is a Christian believer, spiritual maturity will eventually hopefully result in enlightenment regarding the presence of areas of vulnerability within the self. Thus it is possible to learn to intercept and abort attempts at inner manipulation by using a counter-attack of inspired self-knowledge. But in the case of the unbelieving soul or the inwardly unenlightened Christian it is a different story altogether. In such cases the powers of darkness may have a proverbial field day. Malign 'stirring' of the weak spots of wounded individuals commonly occurs in the scope of one-to-one Christian relationships or in the central dynamics of Christian communities. If not nipped in the bud, such activity has the potential to escalate into a raging bonfire of disquiet. In my work as spiritual guide and counselor, I came across many such angst-ridden situations where it became abundantly clear that malign influence was insidiously at work. If such situations remain unchallenged and unchecked, the potential result is chaos. The Christian life, both individually and corporately, therefore consists of a relentless and ongoing spiritual battle on very many levels. While believers may rejoice in the knowledge that all will ultimately be well, it is also necessary to remain constantly 'on the alert'.[11] There can be no half measures in the work of such prayerful vigilance on behalf of oneself and others.

There are some individuals who are specifically called to ministry in the area of spiritual malignancy in various situations. This specialized area has, in recent years, received much hype in the area of the media. The latter is no bad thing as this has served to open up and pinpoint the subject and has introduced much intelligent discussion across the board. Work concerning the powers of darkness should only ever be undertaken by Christians of maturity - those who have plainly been called by God to such a task. In such work one needs to be constantly rooted and grounded in Christ. The charism of exorcism is potentially an extremely dangerous undertaking and one needs to have achieved a high degree of sound inner wholeness even to consider it. In this ministry, if the powers of darkness discern any discrepancy between one's state of inner healedness and one's projected outer persona, they will immediately try to gain a foothold in the negative sense and will attempt to introduce much malign mischief. In this type of work it is essential to operate within a group of similarly gifted individuals and it is something that one should never attempt to grapple with alone. One is also vitally in need of prayer support while undertaking such ministry and afterwards there will be a need to discuss one's experience. In other words, this is not a stand-alone charism. But again this is a very wide and complicated subject and is not something which ultimately falls within the scope of this book. In general, one should always remember that Christ is all powerful and that the utterance of His Name immediately protects the Christian soul from all that is dark and negative. It is true to say that the further one travels into the light of God the less one is prey to attack by evil forces. The dark powers are able to 'suggest' thoughts into our minds when we are on the lower levels of the spiritual journey and are able to 'cloak' these thoughts in false light, so that we perceive them to be coming from a positive source. It is up to us to discern this. If we give the enemy a 'beachhead' by falling into a particular sin, we then bring to ourselves the vulnerability of a wide open door through which further sinful thoughts and temptations may be introduced along the same lines. It is rather like an instance of locking and bolting an entire house, then foolishly leaving one small window open which allows access to an intruder.

Concerning the work of intercession on the earth, there are many Christian souls who work 'underground', as it were, on behalf of God's Kingdom. The deeper levels of contemplative prayer often render it possible to perceive and receive the pain and suffering of others on a hidden level of consciousness. This makes perfect sense of course, for we are all connected and we are all members of one body in Christ. Experienced intercessors are able to 'carry' burdens, on behalf of others, in the short or the long term. But careful discernment should always be implemented before commencing on this costly path, as there is always the inherent danger that one could find oneself horribly out of one's depth. It is true to say that all prayers of intercession carry the essential imprint and identity of the one who prays. In this way, the subjects towards whom one's prayer is directed are not only blessed by God's healing love but also with the unique fragrance of one's own persona. The depth of our prayer and our closeness to God reflects the quality and form of the spiritual blessing that we are able to endow upon others. The action of vicariously lifting the pain of others to God happens in the exactly the same way as the offering of our own issues, grief and burdens to God during prayer.

In the course of intercessory prayer, one initially receives a human need, either directly from the person concerned, from another party, or simply by one's own observation (for those who are in need of prayer are not always aware of the fact). Then, at the earliest possible opportunity, one seeks to take the burden of prayer to God and to leave it there. This 'handing over' to Almighty God is an extremely important point. In one's verve and enthusiasm to be an effective intercessor one should never attempt to 'hold' the pain of others within oneself in some sort of a misguided heroic gesture. Christ alone has the power to deal effectively with all human pain, whatever its shape or form. If, in the course of intercessory prayer, we attempt to hold the pain of others within ourselves, we not only run the risk of overburdening our own psyches and hearts, but ultimately we deny the one we are praying for the help and healing that they can only receive from God. As mentioned earlier, if one is on a spiritual journey of any serious intent, one should seek to make a new and fresh commitment of one's whole self to God on a daily basis. This serves constantly to allow God access to every corner and nuance of our own souls, ensuring that every cell of one's being is perpetually rendered Godward. Thus one places oneself in a position of continually being saturated with the Holy Spirit, which in turn facilitates effective prayerful intercession for others.

Although it is possible to intercede and to vicariously carry pain long term on behalf of others, Christ will sometimes put the brakes on such intercessory suffering. I have a good friend - now here with me on this side of being - who went through the most agonizing turmoil during the time of his wife's death from terminal cancer. At the time, my friend pleaded with God that he himself might be allowed to take his dear wife's pain completely. Indeed, he would have willingly died in her stead; such was the depth of his love and devotion to her. But at the time God appeared completely 'deaf' to his request - a fact which rocked my friend's Christian faith considerably for a period of time. It was only much later that it became clear that my friend had been too wounded to bear such a burden, due to his own need for inner healing from past emotional pain. The details of the case were that during early childhood he had suffered intense emotional trauma at the time of the death of his mother - a pain that he had never acknowledged and had subsequently buried. This had served to hold him back throughout his life on many levels. Exposure to the experience of the agony of loss yet again allowed this early wound to come to the surface, which in turn brought about his inner healing with God's help. So the carrying of a burden of suffering for another is not always possible due to one's own inner fragility. We must trust that God knows each one of us intimately and often much better than we know ourselves. In the general sense, if our lives are completely surrendered to God, He is always working for good on our behalf and on behalf of those for whom we pray. As such we must trust Him in all things implicitly. As St Paul reminds us: 'in everything, as we know, he co-operates for good with those who love God and are called according to his purpose.'[12]

But there are times when God will permit the long term carrying of a physical, emotional or spiritual burden on behalf of another. This specialized and hidden work is carried out by great souls on the earth and also on this side of being. On the earthly level, I refer to the army of intercessors within the religious life, which, when lived impeccably, can have a positively explosive effect on the cosmic consciousness. Such dedicated individuals stand relentlessly in intercession before God. The true results of their hallowed work will not be apparent until we all reach this side of being. But for most of us, by far the best form of intercession is to stand perpetually before God in contemplative adoration, loving Him and being loved by Him. This is the best possible offering that one can make in easing the pain of the world, because it has the potential, macrocosmically, to act for good within the collective consciousness of humankind and serves to lift the whole a little further into the light of God's love. Thus, the further we journey as individuals into the light of God by virtue of our own spiritual progress, the more we are able to contribute to the healing of the collective human consciousness.

Overall, the most effective influence for good in this world, in the context of the guidance and healing of souls, can be said to be wrought by example. In other words, not by 'doing', but by the nature of one's 'being' in the collective dance of human existence. It is not always necessary to be actively 'hands on'. There are many who successfully lead others to Christ by their subtle positive influence and by allowing their individual light to shine within the gloom of the present age. Therefore, within the madrigalian chorus of human existence, one should strive to sing one's song with verve and confidence, because many miracles can be wrought passively. By tending solicitously to the garden of one's own inner life, it is possible to cause positivity to echo through the collective consciousness, resulting in calling others to the path of truth, love and peace. In this way one is able to interweave the tapestry of human pain with one's own distinctive signature threads of bright gold hope.

17.

THE CONCEPTION OF LIFE

From the moment a new life is conceived on the earth, a soul waits in readiness on this side of being. Following a three month gestation period, the soul and the fetus become connected by an etheric cord - in the area of the fetal solar plexus. The soul does not enter the fetus until directly before the moment of birth. During the gestation period, it remains outside of the mother's body in its state of etheric attachment. At the time of conception, an auric shield moves into place around the fetus. During gestation this absorbs the familial characteristics of the life situation the soul is about to enter. Thus, once a child is born, he or she immediately possesses an intrinsic sense of belonging to the family group. The auric shield also holds details of the life that is about to unfold - the 'marching orders', in other words, relating to the soul's coming time on the earth. Each soul has tasks to complete, a journey to negotiate and other souls to interact with. Nothing ever happens by chance. At the very center of the waiting soul is the nucleus that contains the divine spark. This is the soul blueprint - its spiritual 'DNA' and its essential identity in God.

Shortly before the time of birth, the soul moves along the etheric cord and enters the waiting fetus, ready for entry into the world. The waiting soul does not possess conscious awareness until the time of birth, but remains in a state of profound rest. The soul would not survive if it were situated inside the placental sac for the lengthy period of gestation, as it is constantly in need of ions within the atmosphere to recharge its kinetic and psychic energies. There is so much about all of this that is difficult to convey because of the limitations of earthly understanding. There is a virtual 'wall' that prevents my revealing the whole picture, so that I am forced to distil much in order to translate it into earthly terms. Complete understanding is therefore inevitably lost.

I would like to touch briefly on the subject of disability at birth. Few on the earth recognize that disability, both physical and psychological, has an essential part to play in the cosmic dance of life. Indeed, many great and advanced souls choose specifically to be reborn into what many people might regard as a pointless existence. But a life of disability, in whatever form, bears great fruit in the onward struggle of collective existence. All of human life is in the process of creating a cosmic pattern. Those who struggle with disability are in fact the threads of gold within the loom of human life. In order to recognize this, one should try to look more closely and carefully at such people, because many ancient and evolved souls are on the earth completing difficult incarnations of one sort or another. These souls are in the process of pouring special grace into the cosmic consciousness. In general, the human race should not be so concerned with 'outward packaging'. As previously noted, Scripture tells us: 'The Lord does not see as a mortal sees; mortals see only appearances but the Lord sees into the heart.'[1]

There has been much fierce debate in recent years surrounding the area of stem cell research. But these matters cannot be reasoned out solely at the level of the mind. At the very center of any ethical debate is distilled the essence of human dignity and integrity. The field of scientific research is quite literally swarming with angelic presences. Ideas and concepts regarding this delicate area are largely inspired, thank God, by good. There are also many 'devil's advocates' on the earth, in the positive sense. In other words, those who ask awkward questions just at the right time and serve to act as catalysts in keeping this area of research on the straight and narrow, as it were. Such scientific breakthroughs are originally inspired by the Divine, but it is excellent that such care and detailed debate is continually taking place at a human level. Guidelines pertaining to this subject have been arrived at by virtue of an unconscious collaboration between both sides of the curtain. In other words there has been integral spiritual inspiration and intent. In the case of stem cell research, the developing fetuses can be said to be purely 'clinical' with no human soul involved at all. But if they were allowed to develop beyond the agreed watershed, a waiting soul would begin to draw near in readiness simply because we are working by rules here and this is the way it all happens. In the general sense, it is good that much 'policing' is taking place in this whole area. The angels and the higher beings are playing a large part in terms of influence in the development of such work. It is obviously very important that this area should be continually infused with divine light.

To touch briefly on the subject of human cloning and whether this is right or wrong in the eyes of God. The body is essentially a 'vehicle' serving to carry the soul during its journey on the earth. In this sense it really has no more importance than the shape, size, color or model of one's car. Yes, it is obviously altogether more pleasant to travel within a body that is beautiful and perfectly proportioned. But essentially it does not really matter in any sense. What matters is the eternal soul. If one were able to begin cloning the soul then an angry debate would indeed be justified. But this is not, and never will be possible. Physical cloning could result in the earth being populated by a 'super race' of athletic Adonis type figures. This would be all well and good - but these outwardly perfect beings would still contain the fragility that is the human soul. It would, in fact, be more difficult for these beings to make significant and useful progress at soul level, because they would undoubtedly need to get past their enormous egos in the first instance. It is true to say that frailty and brokenness bear the most valuable spiritual fruit.

There has always been much debate on the subject of abortion. The Bible clearly tells us: 'Thou shalt not kill.'[2] All human life is sacred. The body is sacred and is a vessel created by Almighty God. But for those who have had personal involvement in the tragedy of abortion, it is always possible to come to God and to seek His forgiveness. As Scripture says: 'if we confess our sins, he is just and may be trusted to forgive our sins and cleanse us from every kind of wrongdoing.'[3] This is immutable fact. There is always a way back for the sincere of heart and no one should ever despair at all. In the sense of a fetus self-aborting through miscarriage - this passing is expected and is prepared for on this side of being. Provision will already have been made for the safe passage of the soul. But in the case of deliberate abortion after the gestation period of three months - the attached soul will by then be in its place of rest above the mother's body and will be connected by the etheric cord to the developing fetus. It is then that intercessory prayer on the earth is needed to help to guide such souls towards the light of God. A requiem Mass is an extremely effective means of bringing healing and peace in such cases and this should be implemented without delay. Once an aborted or miscarried fetus has reached a place of safety on this side of being there will then follow progression to the plane of childhood and there is a specific receiving area of healing. Such souls initially enter a shallow healing pool that is surrounded by angelic presences. The water within the pool possesses intrinsic healing properties. The water is not static, but ripples gently, rocking the souls as would have been the case during attachment to the body of an earthly mother as she moves about her daily tasks. Around the pool is pleasant greenery - trees and fragrant flowers. Supervisory angels with the purest of faces travel over the surface of the pool at regular intervals, bestowing showers of blessings. At the side of the pool a small group of angels play a constant gentle melody of healing. Divine healing light also shines down constantly upon the pool. When the souls reach a certain stage - the time at which they would have naturally been born on the earth - an attending angel takes them gently from the pool and sits, rocking and comforting in exactly the same way that their natural mother would have done. During the nursing process, the angel's heart repeatedly glows gold and from the heart flows a supply of constant love directly into the heart of the soul in question. After a period of such healing, the soul will then progress on to the plane of childhood and will be tenderly cared for there.

As I mentioned earlier, Marylu, one of our number, is an eternal child and remains in a state of perpetual childhood. There is an essential spiritual reason for this. In the Gospels Our Lord says: 'Let the children come to me; do not try to stop them; for the kingdom of Heaven belongs to such as these.'[4] He adds: 'whoever does not accept the kingdom of God like a child will never enter it.'[5] If one were to compare Marylu's numerical age to that of a child upon the earth, she would be aged around seven years. This was the age of her passing during her last incarnation and is the age at which she will remain on this side of life. All children within the life of eternity occupy a special place within the Father's heart and as such have a unique relationship with Almighty God. They act as spiritual catalysts in the life beyond death and are able to contribute to the greater good in a way that would not be possible in the case of an adult. A child existing in the life of eternity facilitates unique spiritual waves that resound throughout the spheres which are essential for the progression of the Kingdom. As a child soul, Marylu is able to relate to the heart of God in a unique way. As such she receives inner gifts and blessings that she is then able to impart to needy children on the earth plane. Marylu also contributes to the work of AVESHIDA in her own special way. When a child passes over to this side of being, Marylu is far better equipped than any adult soul to minister to their need. This is most especially so, as I mentioned earlier, in the case of a tragic passing - due to violence or some other distressing situation.

Anyone who has had first-hand life experience of the passing of a child or an infant knows only too well the depth of immense grief involved. It is normal to experience intense anger and distress in the face of such experiences, however strong one's faith in God. It seems grossly unjust that a child should be plucked away before he or she has had the opportunity to taste and experience life in all its fullness. But there are souls, of whom Marylu is one, whose very vocation and purpose is to exist upon the earth for a relatively short span. Those who have had personal relationships with such children during their brief journeys on the earth will concur that, in the majority of cases, such children possess what is colloquially known as 'an old head on young shoulders'. In other words, they normally display a maturity of spirit that far exceeds their years in the numerical and developmental sense. The reason for this is that many such children are very old souls. As such, they possess innate wisdom, and while they are not consciously aware that this is the case, those around them will observe it and be constantly surprised by it.

The plane of childhood on this side of being is a gentle place and is populated entirely by the young and those who care for them. The spiritual name of this plane is 'Erchonalia'. Among the carers who choose to work and assist on this plane are those who exhibited natural gifts on the earth of an understanding and rapport with children. There are yet others who were denied the bearing of children themselves while on the earth, or who sustained the trauma of losing a child through death and for whom a period on this plane brings inner healing. Erchonalia is a place of immense beauty, gentleness and quiet joy. There are special areas within the plane for each age group. For instance, there is a specific area for babies and infants who passed over under the age of eighteen months. This is the soft lush meadow of

The Conception of Life

the eternal cradles where the infants are gently rocked and comforted. Here there is an atmosphere of intense peace and goodwill. Each baby is held securely within their own crib and waves of love enfold the area - love that comes directly from the Father's own heart. The aspect which strikes one immediately when first visiting this area is that none of the babies is crying. No baby is distressed in any way whatsoever. This is because they know that they are safe, loved and that all is well. God the Father ministers to each child individually and, as such, it is as if each has a mother in attendance. For God, as many are aware, is both Father and Mother. The babies grow and progress at the normal rate - in exactly the same way as a child upon the earth. The babies remain within the cradles of love until they reach the age of eighteen months. This is essentially an area of suspension of being and is similar to the place in which I spent time during my initial period of healing following my passing over to this side of life. It is an atmosphere of pure love and the babies experience this as a pleasant, dream-like state. The babies will grow and they will progress at the normal rate - in exactly the same way as such a child upon the earth.

After this stage, at the developmental age equal to eighteen months on the earth, the babies progress to a different area within Erchonalia. There is a type of mansion house standing in beautiful grounds and within this house, the children are cared for by the helpers I mentioned earlier on.

In the general sense, one may wonder how one mansion house could possibly hold the vast numbers of children who pass over from the earth plane? Here I need to give a simplistic explanation of the concept of numbers here. Imagine if you will a single grain of sand. Within that grain of sand are many atoms and each atom is intrinsically linked one to another. Then stretch your imagination further to include the concept that, ultimately, each grain of sand collectively forms a beach. Upon that beach the sun shines down and, as the tide moves in and out, the sea saturates the sand with water. Imagine the sun to be the light of God and the sea to be His enfolding love. Such is a simple analogy of the relationship of God with the countless souls inhabiting the spheres in the life beyond death. There are millions of interlocking souls that are all overseen by the light and love of God. There is but one God, one Christ and one Holy Spirit and from their central place of being, they transmit their glorious presence along the 'interconnections', in order to relate individually to each soul. And each soul has within it a divine nucleus that denotes its belonging to Almighty God.

To return to an example of one single mansion house among the many that exist within the plane of childhood. In such dwellings, as I have said, the children live after the age of eighteen months. These are places of laughter, joy and play, infused with the love of God. There is extreme happiness in each mansion house. Of course, there are cases where children have passed over in tragic and distressing circumstances. These are situations where much healing is needed and such children are given sufficient space and time for this to develop. They will receive ministry from souls of light who visit the plane regularly for this specific purpose. A child who is wounded in any way will be allowed as much time as they need to rest and heal. Souls of light will come often to be with the child and will surround them with love and light. Then, when such a child is ready, a soul of light will help them to review their past life in order to bring healing to all that is painful. The child will thus be encouraged to experience emotions and feelings that may be deeply buried. This all happens at a pace and in a timescale that proves manageable for each individual child. No one is in any rush at all on this side of life.

The children passing over who do not have such wounds to address are received into an atmosphere of joy and love and peace. There will be opportunity for reunion with loved ones who have already passed over and, once a child is fully settled, he or she may choose to pass permanently to the place of existence of his or her family unit. Such children will then return to Erchonalia for the purpose of their education. Others may choose to remain constantly within Erchonalia and from there will visit their loved ones when they so desire. There are schools over here and the children have ample opportunity for learning. These are led partly by the carers whom I mentioned earlier and partly by advanced souls of light, who come to teach the children about existence on this side of life. Each child also has a mentor - an advanced soul - who acts as a one-to-one guide. This will be someone who is compatible with the child's essential personality and make-up. Each of us in AVESHIDA is a mentor to a child on the plane of Erchonalia. This is a role that I particularly enjoy, since I was denied the opportunity of fatherhood during my lifetime on the earth.

Life within Erchonalia is not all about work and learning. There is much opportunity for play and Erchonalia itself is a place of great beauty. There are rolling fields and mountains. Seascapes and meadows. Gardens of wondrous flowers. Animals, birds and wildlife. Everything has an altogether educational slant. The children have constant opportunity to learn and this is made possible in an enjoyable way.

I am always reluctant to leave this plane and it warms my heart and gives me joy to share about this wondrous place of light.

18.

THE EONS OF HEALING

On the cusp of the farthest reaches of light there are many-faceted advanced souls consisting of more than one unit. In such cases soul structure is markedly different from the norm. There exists a light-infused mother-soul at the very center and spanning out from the central axis are tributaries, as in a river. The whole concept may be compared to a type of wheel. Attached at the end of each tributary are soul extensions that normally number twelve in all. These individual units have the capacity to be reborn on the earth, for the purpose of the catalytic assistance of humankind. During the whole process, the mother-soul remains within the farthest reaches of light and as such is perpetually saturated and infused with divine light and energy. The soul extensions have the facility to return to the earth one by one in order to enter and participate in various life situations. Their purpose is to exist as a presence of light and truth within human situations of grief, tragedy and pain. Their action is to send out waves of healing within distressing and injurious situations. Their waves of divine love and healing bring succor and strength to individuals, groups and to the collective consciousness as a whole. Once they have been incarnated in this way, the soul extensions assume the same state of 'unknowing' common to all, but as their spiritual journey progresses they may begin to perceive the true nature of their own identity. This whole concept makes it possible to glean a deeper understanding of the doctrine of the Holy Trinity. In this sense, God the Father, within the Holy Trinity, is representative of the mother-soul and God the Son represents His soul extension. The Holy Spirit represents the divine light-filled power that flows osmotically between the Father and the Son.

The same concept occurs in the domain of the powers of darkness. Here again there is a central source that exists in the depths of the lower regions. Again there are tributaries radiating out from the center. The soul extensions at the end of these tributaries are also able to be born in bodily form upon the earth. These are those who act as catalysts of darkness, bringing great distress to many on the earth in dark periods of human history. But their insidious power may be lessened and nullified through the ardent prayer of the faithful elect on the earth.

At the very beginning of time the mother-soul first starts its existence in a state of lone individuality. It is only after many eons of spiritual evolution that such a soul reaches the Seventh Level of existence. He or she is then given the option of proceeding onwards towards complete absorption into the light of God, thereafter becoming Christified and one of the elect. Or the said soul may make the choice of holding back in order to be of assistance to the world and to humankind. If the latter choice is made, the mother-soul remains poised on the cusp between the greater light of God and the relatively lesser light of the Seventh Level. It becomes privy to the knowledge of the deepest secrets of God and is able to collude with higher echelons of light.

During their lifetimes on the earth, many people proffer the question that if an all-powerful God exists, why does He not prevent tragic situations occurring collectively and individually on the earth? The answer to this question is that humankind itself is entirely responsible for the writing and unfolding of its own destiny. All human darkness and pain is caused by individual and collective turning away, over a long period of time, from the path of light and love. All situations of pain and misfortune on the earth are not vented passively by some sort of a despotic god, but are self-inflicted. At the present time, humankind is perpetually engaged in the act of self-injecting its own suffering into its own veins. Every selfish, cruel and dark deed or action, large or small, committed on the earth has the knock-on effect of giving birth to an identical occurrence elsewhere on the planet. On the opposite end of the scale, acts and attitudes of kindness and charity perpetuate the fragrant blooming of love and peace in other parts of the globe. The human race is corporately interlinked and is constantly weaving its own collective pattern. The tendency of relegating blame and the assertion that God is responsible for the darkness in the world really constitutes a childish shirking of responsibility. Humankind needs to take collective responsibility for its own situation. The gift of free will means that the human race is responsible for deciding, moment by moment, the course in which it is headed. A juvenile, petulant railing towards God about every unfortunate situation that exists on the earth reflects the essential innate immaturity of the human race. Only by looking into its collective heart will humankind ultimately find the answers it seeks. If, as now, it persists in constantly straying from paths of love, light and truth and continues to dip its proverbial toe into every imaginable evil, it should not be at all surprised by the fact that its world is collapsing into a state of disintegration: morally, emotionally, spiritually and physically. Everything has consequences and this is something that we all need to learn on a personal level from our very infancy. Such is also the case corporately and globally. If the human race were collectively to forge a new path based on love, light and peace, then harmony would begin to be restored and the earth would gradually start to heal itself from its current ecological and ethical suicide. At present the human race collectively resembles the mentality of a fractious and destructive toddler, with a penchant for self-abuse and abuse of the natural world in which it exists. It is amazing that humankind constantly remains surprised about the nature of the self-made bed upon which it is lying.

Regarding the question of predestination, it is necessary to examine the concept of time versus eternity. There is no time in eternity and this basically means that the future, the past and the present are all on one level and are occurring at exactly the same moment in the virtual sense. If any change to any part of the pattern occurs - for better or for worse - the whole pattern is instantly rewoven. It is well-nigh impossible to properly explain this concept within the bounds of finite understanding, because the boundaries of time in the earthly consciousness create so many insurmountable blockages to understanding. What I am trying to convey is that change, for the better (or ultimately for the worse) is possible. All is not lost. Despite the darkness that exists at the present time in human history and the pain of the memories of darkness in the past, at the moment all is ultimately redeemable. The key is Jesus Christ. He is the catalyst and He has the ability to unlock the potentiality of change in the world as it exists today. Only by an individual and corporate embracing of the truth of Christ's Cross can healing come about. The Cross of Christ has the power to change the current pattern on the loom which humankind itself is weaving. But time is short. The necessary changes must come about soon.

The initial state of the individual soul is that of an empty book on which the experiences of life have yet to be written. At the very center of each soul there exists a divine spark that waits in readiness to be kindled into a flame if the choice is made to turn to God. Enclosing and surrounding the central divine spark is the human ego or will, which initially is the centrifugal force around which all else revolves. At the very beginning of the history of humankind, the two primary souls - Adam and Eve, stood poised at the crossroads of existence. In one direction lay glory, joy and peace and the potential to permit the true light of Almighty God to be their all-pervading focus. In the other direction lay the spiritually restrictive qualities of the human will or ego. The fact that the latter course was chosen meant that henceforth all else flowed from a fractured and distorted base. The end result was that subsequent members of the human race inherited an existence that oscillated imperfectly around the false light of the collective ego. At the present time, humankind can be said to be progressing through an age of potentially redemptive shadow. Countless souls on the earth are very far from God and from the truth. Within every religious belief on the face of the earth there exists a kernel of the essential truth. God Almighty - however He is termed or named - is supreme over all. God is Spirit - the Spirit of love. He is all-seeing and all-knowing. He is the Creator of everything that is. He is endless and He is formless. He is actually neither he nor she but I am using the term 'He' for ease of understanding.

There are very many worlds and we of this universe are not all that exists. But it is of very little use to travel in the conventional sense in a never-ending quest to discover others in our own galaxy. The ones that we seek can never be discovered in this way. Space travel has, of course, reaped many rewards scientifically and no sincere human effort is without its uses and its positive ends. But ultimately, travel to other universes and worlds may only take place as a result of successfully journeying to the very center of our beings. There exists a parallel universe in line with this one. And in line with this second universe is another. Each universe exists in the center of the other. This renders space travel and investigation utterly void. Such outward journeying will bear no fruit at all. Only by travelling inward will humankind make significant discoveries and find answers. And the way to the inner journey is prayer and meditation as advocated by the major religions. Within oneself is all that has been created and all that is not created - that which is divine. This goes on forever into eternity and beyond. There is no ending and no beginning. There is only infinity and perpetuation and everlasting life. This is the only way forward and this will open the door. Here - within our very selves - are the answers we seek. As Our Lord said: 'Enter by the narrow gate. Wide is the gate and broad the road that leads to destruction, and many enter that way; narrow is the gate and constricted the road that leads to life, and those who find them are few.'[1] We ourselves - in terms of our very souls - are the potential key to entering worlds other than our own.

There is an age to come and this will follow the Second Coming of the Lord Jesus Christ. At this time the present earth as we know it will be no more and there will be a second earth and a completely new dimension of time and space. On this new earth will be those who have the Name of the Lamb inscribed upon their foreheads. At this time, those who have perpetually turned away from Almighty God and the cause of light will be no more - they who have followed the antichrist, the fiend or prince of darkness. At the very end of all time the serpent will rise from the seas - he who is called Satan. A great battle will follow and there will be clashing of swords and spears. Those among the angelic hosts - the Powers, Principalities, Rulers, Thrones, Cherubim and Seraphim - all within the force of light and within the company of Almighty God will rise up with a great shout. Michael - he who is the prince of all angels - will be at the fore. This fight will at first be invisible to earthly eyes but will have the effect of inflicting great repercussions on humankind. It will emit waves of profound discontent and the utmost of evil. It will cause the seas to rise, mountains to topple and the heavenly hosts of stars and planets to come tumbling down. But those who are inscribed on the palms of God's hands - those who have been faithful in following the King - will be safe. Darkness will be divided from light upon the earth. He who is not of God will be separated from he who is of God. At this time, the King of Glory will appear on a chariot of light, with His rearing steeds of silver and gold. His aura will stretch out to encompass the ailing earth and He will proceed to spread the most comforting of balms. Behind Him will follow a train of winnowing angels whose task it will be to gather the faithful elect and to bring them home to the light. No fear is necessary and no anxiety is due to those who belong to God - this I must stress. When this will happen and when this should be expected - all that I can say is that it is soon - very soon. The earth is close to reaching its final hour and the signs have been apparent for some time. All I can say is that there is an urgency to repent - because the hour is nigh and there is really very little time left.

Following this will be an age of no more strife and this will be the beginning of the eons of healing. During this age, the proverbial lion will lie with the lamb. At this time there will be a new heaven and a new earth. All that is now in existence will pass away and will become dust. Evil and darkness will be no more. And this will be the beginning of the glorious eons of light. Some may question the ultimate position of those who presently do not hold Almighty God to be supreme over all. Those who deny the Kingship of Our Lord Jesus Christ. The answer to this question lies in purity of heart and individual intent concerning the causes of light and love and peace. Is not love another name for God? Therefore those who are on the side of the cause of love will not be deemed to be against Our Lord. Did not Our Lord say: 'He who is not against us is on our side,'[2] and again: 'there are other sheep of mine, not belonging to this fold.'[3] There are many of other beliefs who possess hearts of pure gold and whose light shines brightly for all to see. You will know of those of whom I speak if you use the eyes of your inmost hearts to discern the truth. Do not make the mistake again of division and persecution as of ages past. That which led to atrocities beyond human thought and description. There are many that humankind, from earliest times, has habitually blighted and rejected. Those whom even the supposed pillars of the Church continue to thwart with unashamed bigotry, rejection and exclusion. Shame on you who act in this way - for ultimately it is you, the persecutors, who will be cast away by God if you do not quickly realize the error of your ways and repent from your lack of essential love before the final hour. You should turn now, before it is too late.

Once those who belong to the Lamb have safely been gathered and retrieved, they will then be led to a vast lighted sphere of safety. From there, all will witness the final destruction of the former heaven and earth. At the appointed time the seas will fully rise and will once again cover the earth. The sky will darken and will turn to blood. All of the planets will tumble and fall. Lightning will flash and thunder will roar. The serpent will rise from the deepest of seas, and the final conflict will commence for all to see. There will be clash of sword upon sword as the devil and his minions exert their final struggle against the forces of light and peace. At this time, Michael and his angelic train will defeat the powers of darkness for all eternity. At the last, with a barely perceptible sigh, the earth will pass away and will be no more. But those who are in the place of safety upon the sphere of everlasting light will be gathered into the heart of God. They will be led to an abode entirely new. The time of this happening is knowledge to which I myself am not privy. But for now, we within the spheres of light pray and intercede for the cause of righteousness and truth, with many tears. We implore you, who have a mind to, turn to God before it is too late. For there will come a time very soon when the door will finally close and there will be no more opportunity to turn and to repent. Seek - seek the light that dwells within your hearts. Seek to follow the cause of truth. This is indeed the only way.

As I have said, in the age to come the lion will lie with the lamb and great peace will reign. All those in existence on the newly formed earth will conform to a specific stage of actualization of essential being. Evil will be no more. There will be a veritable utopia of existence. Yet this will not be 'heaven' in the accepted sense. This will be a lower stage in the scheme of all that is. Man will marry woman and woman will marry man. Procreation will continue to occur. There will be no more war and no more strife. The darkness that has been apparent on the former earth will not exist. There will be a general striving for a higher level of consciousness. There will be access to new worlds and travel will occur to these new worlds. Much learning will take place. There will be no more disease or death in the accepted sense. But there will be an aging process, just as there always has been. The aged will be revered for the nature of their sapiential knowledge. There will be a passing and a moving on but not in the sense of pain and bodily travail as is presently the case. When one has reached a certain age of seniority this will take place. There will be great ones - the higher echelons of light who will move among the inhabitants of the new earth, teaching all that there is to know, as much as each soul is sensibly able to absorb. There will be enjoyment of all that is on the new earth - plant life, the animal world, the lights in the skies (of which glory the aurora borealis, the bows in the skies and the sun setting and rising is a foretaste), the seas, the mountains - such glory that you cannot now imagine. For all that is beauteous and wonderful will have evolved to its greatest height and perfection of being. Within the hearts of humankind at that time will be the light of God Almighty. No darkness will be found in the human heart, but instead there will be an evolving light. The light of all being. Each will be individual, each will differ from the other and will be unique in his or her own glory. Oh how wonderful will be the time of the eons of greater healing.

In this new world there will be teaching of the way of love. The way of contemplation of Almighty God. Humankind will be taught the things of heaven. Psychic and inter-kinetic energy will be manifested and will come to the fore. The earth will be stilled from the chatter of machine and the roar of engine and the thunder of jet propulsion. All will be quiet and all will be still. Nature will come into its own. Humankind will enjoy a natural existence and will live in harmony with all that inhabits the earth. Every species in existence, even those which have currently failed to be, will once again be in evidence, save for those of times long past. I speak of all of the beauty that has existed in the present age of humankind. Birds and flowers, creatures on land and sea - all will be manifested, even those thought to be long lost. This will be a time of great joy and of peace and will be a preparation for the even greater ages that are to come. There will not yet be travel to other worlds - until humankind has undergone a period of consolidation of being. Such travel and interaction will be long hence and something that will come in a future Age of humankind. But there will be an implanting of higher souls who will teach and guide in the ways of light. There will be schooling in such skills as the transfer of thought and the interaction of existence within cohesive groups of one sort or another - the ways of love, the ways of truth and of light. In this place of light, a new intelligence will come into being, for the power that will be drawn on and the power which will fuel all things will be a combination of the powers of light and love. There will be no more war, there will be no more hunger and there will be no more need of any kind. The human form will be the same as it always has been, but because of the centrality of love it will proceed to function in an optimum way. There will be no more disease and each organism from the largest to the smallest will function in a positive way. In removing the source of evil in the world, the way ahead will be forged to perfect harmony of being. A cohesive interaction will exist between all living things and all races and cultures will come into their own, with a sense of dignity and actuality that has been glimpsed but has never been attained in this present world. All beings will be celebrated. Music and the arts will flourish. All that is positive will blossom and thrive. Eventually there will be travel to other worlds. For humankind in its present state of inherent darkness is not worthy of such a privilege and this way has previously always been closed. Yet those of other worlds have made contact while keeping their distance - as those in authority on the present earth already know full well. But these matters are kept in wraps to prevent a general panic in any sense. Yet there is nothing to fear. For the power of light surrounds and protects this world even in its present meager spiritual state.

The time will come when AVESHIDA as a group will move onward beyond the Seventh Plane of existence. At that time the group members will no longer retain an autonomous and separate state, and, while not losing our essential individuality, we will become one. There will be a synaptic interfusion between each soul and the energy and force giving rise to this exchange will be the power of love. AVESHIDA will then become a structural cell formed of our group of souls in which the hearts and minds of each interact with love. They will eventually become aligned with the Divine and will ultimately be a part of the divine energy of love. The soul extensions remaining in earthly existence will also receive a divine interchange - back and forth, to and fro - in a constant osmotic exchange of pure, pure love. So it was with the Christ. While He was implanted on the earth His heart constantly interacted both with His Father in Heaven and with the communion of saints, back and forth, to and fro. This created synapses of the divine energy of love - that which is the Holy Spirit. Christ created the initial doorway and implanted the possibility that this could occur in others who followed Him. Thus the possibility of divine intervention in the finite world was enabled. This is all to do with the energy of love. For the force of love is the greatest of the earth's resources. Love has the potential to conquer all and to achieve all. Humankind should forget forays into space and should concentrate solely on love. For this is the way forward. Humankind's journey is not outward but inward - into the human heart. There is so much to achieve, so much to discover here - the interconnectedness between each heart. The communion of heart which can only take place within the kernel of love in existence therein. Thus, within one's heart one can interconnect with all souls living and 'dead' and one can begin to access and absorb the answer to all things. The solution to all things is love!! This is what all of us without exception are aiming at. This is what the interrelatedness between individuals within earthly existence is ultimately all about. This is why Scripture constantly exhorts us to love one another, because, at a certain point in eternity we will form one body with those souls to whom we are close. Once our relationships are perfected we will then travel on into God with our companions in the spirit - those whom we have formed love relationships on the earth.

And so I will now close this epistle and I will leave you with these thoughts. I will communicate further with more about this greatest of all adventures. But for the present, we of AVESHIDA send numerous blessings of light, love and peace!

I remain your servant,
Martin Israel.
In the Name
of Jesus Christ,
Our Lord and Savior,
AMEN.

December 2012

NOTES

Introductory Quotation:
 Lewis, C.S. (1964), *Prayer: Letters to Malcolm*. Glasgow: Fount. p.123.

Foreword
 1 Dorothy Kerin (1889 - 1963) was a British Christian mystic with a ministry of healing.

Martin Israel: A Short Biography
 1 Walter, J.B. and M. S. Israel. (1963), *General Pathology*. London: J. and A. Churchill.

1. Passing
 1 1 Corinthians 13.12.
 2 Psalm 89.2. (New Jerusalem Bible).

2. Coming Home
 1 Luke 1.38.

3. The Group Soul
 1 Greaves, H. (1969), *Testimony of Light*. Saffron Walden: Neville Spearman Publishers.
 2 Romans 12.4-5.
 3 John 14.2.
 4 1 Corinthians 13.12.
 5 Psalm 68.6. (New Jerusalem Bible).
 6 Genesis 2.18.

4. My Own Road to Calvary
 1 See Bibliography for details of Martin Israel's written works.

5. The Nature of Forgiveness
 1 Luke 23.34.
 2 Matthew 19.14, Mark 10.14, Luke 18.16.
 3 Matthew 18.6.
 4 Lewis, C.S. (1960), *The Four Loves*. London: Fount.
 5 Luke 1.37. (New Jerusalem Bible).
 6 Hebrews 13.8.

7. Further In
 1 Matthew 27.46, Mark 15.34.

2 John 20.14.
3 Luke 24.16.
4 Luke 24.30.
8. The Miracle of the Atonement
1 Acts 9.3-6.
2 Deuteronomy 33.27. (KJV)
3 Matthew 27.46, Mark 15.34.
4 Genesis 22.1-14.
5 Matthew 27.51, Mark 15.38, Luke 23.45.
9. The Eternal Legacy
1 The belief that the Eucharistic elements of bread and wine become the body and blood of Christ at consecration, while the outward appearances remain the same.
2 Acts 2.2-4.
10. The Hidden Treasure
1 Genesis 3.1-7.
2 Matthew 13.45-46.
3 Lewis, C.S. (1940), *The Problem of Pain*. Glasgow: Fount. p.74.
11. True Prayer (1)
1 Matthew 13.45-46.
2 Instruction on praying the Rosary may be found in: Neville Ward, J. (1993), *Five For Sorrow, Ten For Joy: Consideration of the Rosary, (New Ed Edition)*. London. Darton, Longman and Todd Ltd.
Instruction on praying the Jesus Prayer may be found in:
Ware, K. (1974), *The Power of the Name: The Jesus Prayer In Orthodox Spirituality*. Oxford: SLG Press.
3 Chapman, J. (Ed. R. Hudleston). (1935), *The Spiritual Letters of Dom John Chapman O.S.B.* London: Sheed and Ward. p.25.
4 Cohen, J. M. (trans.), (1957), *The Life of St Teresa of Ávila By Herself*. Harmondsworth: Penguin Books Ltd. ch.8.p.63.
5 Mark 10.15, Luke 18.17.

6 Monnin, A. (1907), *Life of the Blessed Curé D'Ars*. London: Burns, Oates and Washbourne. p.47.
7 1 Kings 19.12. (KJV)
8 Matthew 7.13-14.

12. True Prayer (2)
1 Luke 10.38-42.
2 Romans 12.4-6.
3 Lewis, C.S. (Ed. Walter Hooper), (1979), *God in the Dock: Essays on Theology*. London: Fount. p.112.
4 Jeremiah 17.9.
5 Jay, E. (ed.), (1987), *The Journal of John Wesley: A Selection*. Oxford: Oxford University Press.
6 Galatians 2.20.
7 John 8.32.
8 Revelation 1.8.
9 Matthew 5.8.

13. The Spirit Filled Life
1 John 14.26.
2 Matthew 7.7, Luke 11.9.
3 Matthew 5.22-24.
4 Revelation 3.20.
5 Excerpt from the hymn: *Come Holy Ghost Our Souls Inspire*. R.Maurus, (c776-856) then J.Cosin, (1594-1672).
6 I Corinthians 12.7.
7 I Corinthians 12.8-11.
8 I Corinthians 12.4-6.
9 I Corinthians 13.1-3,13.
10 Genesis 1.2.
11 Galatians 5.22.
12 2 Corinthians 3.18.
13 Excerpt from the hymn: *Love Divine, All Loves Excelling*. Charles Wesley (1707-1788).

14. Psychic Sensitivity (1)
1 Matthew 26.36-46, Mark 14.32-42, Luke 22.39-46.
2 Matthew 4.1-11, Mark 1.12-13, Luke 4.1-13.
3 Ephesians 6.11-17.

15. Psychic Sensitivity (2)
1 See Chapter 11, note 2.
2 Lewis, C.S. (1956), *The Last Battle*. Harmondsworth: Penguin Books. p.135.

16. Lighting the Path
1 1 Corinthians 1.27-28.
2 Jeremiah 1.6.
3 Jeremiah 1.7.
4 1 Samuel 16.7.
5 Isaiah 42.6-7.
6 An excellent and informative book for further reading on this subject is:
McAll, K. (1986), *Healing the Family Tree*. London: Sheldon Press.
7 Matthew 9.12, Mark 2.17, Luke 5.31.
8 Luke 4.23.
9 Matthew 7.15.
10 Philippians 4.8.
11 I Peter 5.8.
12 Romans 8.28.

17. The Conception of Life
1 1 Samuel 16.7.
2 Exodus 20.13. (KJV).
3 I John 1.9.
4 Matthew 19.14, Mark 10.14, Luke 18.16.
5 Mark 10.15, Luke 18.17.

18. The Eons of Healing
1 Matthew 7.13-14.
2 Mark 9.40.
3 John 10.16.

BIBLIOGRAPHY

Books by Martin Israel

Israel, Martin. (1974), *Summons to Life: The Search for Identity Through the Spiritual*. London: Hodder and Stoughton Ltd.

Israel, Martin. (1976), *Precarious Living: The Path to Life*. Oxford: Mowbray.

Israel, Martin. (1981), *The Pain That Heals: The Place of Suffering in the Growth of the Person*. London: Hodder and Stoughton Ltd.

Israel, Martin. (1982), *Living Alone: The Inward Journey to Fellowship*. London: SPCK.

Israel, Martin. (1983), *The Spirit of Counsel: Spiritual Perspectives in the Counseling Process*. London: Hodder and Stoughton Ltd.

Israel, Martin. (1984), *Healing as Sacrament: The Sanctification of the World*. London: Darton, Longman and Todd Ltd.

Israel, Martin. (1985), *The Discipline of Love: Ten Commandments for Today*. London: SPCK.

Israel, Martin. (1986), *Coming in Glory: Christ's Presence in the World Today*. London: Darton, Longman and Todd Ltd.

Israel, Martin. (1987), *Gethsemane: The Transfiguring Love - Lent Book*. London: Fount.

Israel, Martin. (1988), *The Pearl of Great Price: Journey to the Kingdom*. London: SPCK.

Israel, Martin. (1989), *The Dark Face of Reality: A Study of Emergent Awareness*. London: Fount.

Israel, Martin. (1989), *The Quest For Wholeness*. London: Darton, Longman and Todd Ltd.

Israel, Martin. (1989), *Creation: The Consummation of the World*. London: Zondervan.

Israel, Martin. (1990), *Night Thoughts*. London: SPCK.

Israel, Martin. (1990), *A Light on the Path: An Exploration of Integrity through the Psalms*. London: Darton, Longman and Todd Ltd.

Israel, Martin. (1993), *Life Eternal*. London: SPCK.

Israel, Martin. (1993), *Smouldering Fire: The Work of the Holy Spirit*. Berkhamsted: Arthur James Ltd.
Israel, Martin. (1995), *Angels: Messengers of Grace*. London: SPCK.
Israel, Martin. (1995), *Dark Victory: Through Depression to Hope*. London: Mowbray.
Israel, Martin. (1997), *Exorcism*. London: SPCK.
Israel, Martin. (1997), *Doubt: The Way of Growth*. London: Continuum International Publishing Group.
Israel, Martin. (1999), *Happiness That Lasts*. London: Continuum International Publishing Group.
Israel, Martin with Neil Broadbent. (2001), *The Devout Life: William Law's Understanding of Divine Love*. London: Mowbray.
Israel, Martin with Neil Broadbent. (2001), *Learning to Love*. London: Mowbray.

Books With Other Authors

Israel, Martin et al. (1993). *How I Pray*. London: Darton, Longman and Todd Ltd.
Appleton, George and Martin Israel. (1995). *The Pocket Oxford Book of Prayer*. Oxford University Press.
Professional Publications
Walter, J.B. and M. S. Israel. (1963). *General Pathology*. London: J. and A. Churchill.

Other Sources of Information

The Churches' Fellowship for Psychical and Spiritual Studies holds a large number of publications by Martin Israel, including booklets and recorded tapes of his lectures.

For further details contact:

The Churches' Fellowship for Psychical and Spiritual Studies, The Rural Workshop,
South Road, North Somercotes, Nr Louth, Lincs.
LN11 7PT.
Website Address:
http://www.churchesfellowship.co.uk

Downloads

Many of Martin Israel's books are available for download on the following website:
http://www.martinisrael.u-net.com/

Printed in Great Britain
by Amazon.co.uk, Ltd.,
Marston Gate.